THE PELICAN SHAKESPEARE
GENERAL EDITORS

STEPHEN ORGEL
A. R. BRAUNMULLER

The Sonnets

135

WHo euer hath her wiſh,thou haſt thy *Will*,
  And *Will* too boote,and *Will* in ouer-plus,
More then enough am I that vexe thee ſtill,
To thy ſweet will making addition thus.
Wilt thou whoſe will is large and ſpatious,
Not once vouchſafe to hide my will in thine,
Shall will in others ſeeme right gracious,
And in my will no faire acceptance ſhine:
The ſea all water,yet receiues raine ſtill,
And in aboundance addeth to his ſtore,
So thou beeing rich in *Will* adde to thy *Will*,
One will of mine to make thy large *Will* more.
  Let no vnkinde,no faire beſeechers kill,
  Thinke all but one,and me in that one *Will*.

The playfully autobiographical (and wittily obscene)
Sonnet 135 in its original form in the 1609 quarto, a good
example of the ambiguities of early modern typography.

William Shakespeare

The Sonnets

EDITED BY STEPHEN ORGEL

**WITH AN INTRODUCTION
BY JOHN HOLLANDER**

PENGUIN BOOKS

PENGUIN BOOKS

Published by the Penguin Group

Penguin Group (USA) Inc., 375 Hudson Street, New York, New York 10014, U.S.A.

Penguin Group (Canada), 90 Eglinton Avenue East, Suite 700, Toronto,
Ontario, Canada M4P 2Y3 (a division of Pearson Penguin Canada Inc.)

Penguin Books Ltd, 80 Strand, London WC2R 0RL, England

Penguin Ireland, 25 St Stephen's Green, Dublin 2, Ireland (a division of Penguin Books Ltd)

Penguin Group (Australia), 250 Camberwell Road, Camberwell,
Victoria 3124, Australia (a division of Pearson Australia Group Pty Ltd)

Penguin Books India Pvt Ltd, 11 Community Centre, Panchsheel Park,
New Delhi – 110 017, India

Penguin Group (NZ), 67 Apollo Drive, Rosedale, North Shore,
Auckland 0745, New Zealand (a division of Pearson New Zealand Ltd)

Penguin Books (South Africa) (Pty) Ltd, 24 Sturdee Avenue,
Rosebank, Johannesburg 2196, South Africa

Penguin Books Ltd, Registered Offices: 80 Strand, London WC2R 0RL, England

The Sonnets edited by Douglas Bush published in the
United States of America in Penguin Books 1961
Revised edition published 1970
This new edition edited by Stephen Orgel with an Introduction
by John Hollander published 2001

15   17   19   20   18   16

Copyright © Penguin Books Inc., 1961, 1970
Copyright © Penguin Putnam Inc., 2001
All rights reserved

LIBRARY OF CONGRESS CATALOGING IN PUBLICATION DATA
Shakespeare, William, 1564–1616.
The sonnets / William Shakespeare ;
edited by Stephen Orgel ; with an introduction by John Hollander.
p.   cm. –(The Pelican Shakespeare)
ISBN 978-0-14-071453-1 (pbk.)
1. Sonnets, English.   I. Orgel, Stephen.   II. Title.   III. Series.
PR2848.A2 075 2001
821'.3—dc21   2001033200

Printed in the United States of America
Set in Adobe Garamond
Designed by Virginia Norey

Contents

Publisher's Note

IT IS ALMOST half a century since the first volumes of the Pelican Shakespeare appeared under the general editorship of Alfred Harbage. The fact that a new edition, rather than simply a revision, has been undertaken reflects the profound changes textual and critical studies of Shakespeare have undergone in the past twenty years. For the new Pelican series, the texts of the plays and poems have been thoroughly revised in accordance with recent scholarship, and in some cases have been entirely reedited. New introductions and notes have been provided in all the volumes. But the new Shakespeare is also designed as a successor to the original series; the previous editions have been taken into account, and the advice of the previous editors has been solicited where it was feasible to do so.

Shakespeare:
The Life and the Texts

WILLIAM SHAKESPEARE OF
STRATFORD-UPON-AVON, GENTLEMAN

MANY PEOPLE have said that we know very little about William Shakespeare's life – pinheads and postcards are often mentioned as appropriately tiny surfaces on which to record the available information. More imaginatively and perhaps more correctly, Ralph Waldo Emerson wrote, "Shakespeare is the only biographer of Shakespeare. . . . So far from Shakespeare's being the least known, he is the one person in all modern history fully known to us."

In fact, we know more about Shakespeare's life than we do about almost any other English writer's of his era. His last will and testament (dated March 25, 1616) survives, as do numerous legal contracts and court documents involving Shakespeare as principal or witness, and parish records in Stratford and London. Shakespeare appears quite often in official records of King James's royal court, and of course Shakespeare's name appears on numerous title pages and in the written and recorded words of his literary contemporaries Robert Greene, Henry Chettle, Francis Meres, John Davies of Hereford, Ben Jonson, and many others. Indeed, if we make due allowance for the bloating of modern, run-of-the-mill bureaucratic records, more information has survived over the past four hundred years about William Shakespeare of Stratford-upon-Avon, Warwickshire, than is likely to survive in the next four hundred years about any reader of these words.

What we do not have are entire categories of information – Shakespeare's private letters or diaries, drafts and revisions of poems and plays, critical prefaces or essays, commendatory verse for other writers' works, or instructions guiding his fellow actors in their performances, for instance – that we imagine would help us understand and appreciate his surviving writings. For all we know, many such data never existed as written records. Many literary and theatrical critics, not knowing what might once have existed, more or less cheerfully accept the situation; some even make a theoretical virtue of it by claiming that such data are irrelevant to understanding and interpreting the plays and poems.

So, what do we know about William Shakespeare, the man responsible for thirty-seven or perhaps more plays, more than 150 sonnets, two lengthy narrative poems, and some shorter poems?

While many families by the name of Shakespeare (or some variant spelling) can be identified in the English Midlands as far back as the twelfth century, it seems likely that the dramatist's grandfather, Richard, moved to Snitterfield, a town not far from Stratford-upon-Avon, sometime before 1529. In Snitterfield, Richard Shakespeare leased farmland from the very wealthy Robert Arden. By 1552, Richard's son John had moved to a large house on Henley Street in Stratford-upon-Avon, the house that stands today as "The Birthplace." In Stratford, John Shakespeare traded as a glover, dealt in wool, and lent money at interest; he also served in a variety of civic posts, including "High Bailiff," the municipality's equivalent of mayor. In 1557, he married Robert Arden's youngest daughter, Mary. Mary and John had four sons – William was the oldest – and four daughters, of whom only Joan outlived her most celebrated sibling. William was baptized (an event entered in the Stratford parish church records) on April 26, 1564, and it has become customary, without any good factual support, to suppose he was born on April 23, which happens to be the feast day of Saint George, patron saint of England, and is also the date on which he died, in 1616. Shakespeare married Anne Hathaway in 1582, when he was eighteen and she was twenty-six; their first child was born five months later. It has been generally assumed that the marriage was enforced and subsequently unhappy, but these are only assumptions; it has been estimated, for instance, that up to one third of Elizabethan brides were pregnant when they married. Anne and William Shakespeare had three children: Susanna, who married a prominent local physician, John Hall; and the twins Hamnet, who died young in 1596, and Judith, who married Thomas Quiney – apparently a rather shady individual. The name Hamnet was unusual but not unique: he and his twin sister were named for their godparents, Shakespeare's neighbors Hamnet and Judith Sadler. Shakespeare's father died in 1601 (the year of *Hamlet*), and Mary Arden Shakespeare died in 1608 (the year of *Coriolanus*). William Shakespeare's last surviving direct descendant was his granddaughter Elizabeth Hall, who died in 1670.

Between the birth of the twins in 1585 and a clear reference to Shakespeare as a practicing London dramatist in Robert Greene's sensationalizing, satiric pamphlet, *Greene's Groatsworth of Wit* (1592), there is no record of where William Shakespeare was or what he was doing. These seven so-called lost years have been imaginatively filled by scholars and other students of Shakespeare: some think he traveled to Italy, or fought in the Low Countries, or studied law or medicine, or worked as an apprentice actor/writer, and so on to even more fanciful possibilities. Whatever the biographical facts for those "lost" years, Greene's nasty remarks in 1592 testify to professional envy and to the fact that Shakespeare already had a successful career in London. Speaking to his fellow playwrights, Greene warns both generally and specifically:

. . . trust them [actors] not: for there is an upstart crow, beautified with our feathers, that with his tiger's heart wrapped in a player's hide supposes he is as well able to bombast out a blank verse as the best of you; and being an absolute Johannes Factotum, is in his own conceit the only Shake-scene in a country.

The passage mimics a line from *3 Henry VI* (hence the play must have been performed before Greene wrote) and seems to say that "Shake-scene" is both actor and playwright, a jack-of-all-trades. That same year, Henry Chettle protested Greene's remarks in *Kind-Heart's Dream,* and each of the next two years saw the publication of poems – *Venus and Adonis* and *The Rape of Lucrece,* respectively – publicly ascribed to (and dedicated by) Shakespeare. Early in 1595 he was named as one of the senior members of a prominent acting company, the Lord Chamberlain's Men, when they received payment for court performances during the 1594 Christmas season.

Clearly, Shakespeare had achieved both success and reputation in London. In 1596, upon Shakespeare's application, the College of Arms granted his father the now-familiar coat of arms he had taken the first steps to obtain almost twenty years before, and in 1598, John's son – now permitted to call himself "gentleman" – took a 10 percent share in the new Globe playhouse. In 1597, he bought a substantial bourgeois house, called New Place, in Stratford – the garden remains, but Shakespeare's house, several times rebuilt, was torn down in 1759 – and over the next few years Shakespeare spent large sums buying land and making other investments in the town and its environs. Though he worked in London, his family remained in Stratford, and he seems always to have considered Stratford the home he would eventually return to. Something approaching a disinterested appreciation of Shakespeare's popular and professional status appears in Francis Meres's *Palladis Tamia* (1598), a not especially imaginative and perhaps therefore persuasive record of literary reputations. Reviewing contemporary English writers, Meres lists the titles of many of Shakespeare's plays, including one not now known, *Love's Labor's Won,* and praises his "mellifluous & hony-tongued" "sugred Sonnets," which were then circulating in manuscript (they were first collected in 1609). Meres describes Shakespeare as "one of the best" English playwrights of both comedy and tragedy. In *Remains . . . Concerning Britain* (1605), William Camden – a more authoritative source than the imitative Meres – calls Shakespeare one of the "most pregnant witts of these our times" and joins him with such writers as Chapman, Daniel, Jonson, Marston, and Spenser. During the first decades of the seventeenth century, publishers began to attribute numerous play quartos, including some non-Shakespearean ones, to Shakespeare, either by name or initials, and we may assume that they deemed Shakespeare's name and supposed authorship, true or false, commercially attractive.

For the next ten years or so, various records show Shakespeare's dual career as playwright and man of the theater in London, and as an important local figure in Stratford. In 1608-9 his acting company – designated the "King's Men" soon after King James had succeeded Queen Elizabeth in 1603 – rented, refurbished, and opened a small interior playing space, the Blackfriars theater, in London, and Shakespeare was once again listed as a substantial sharer in the group of proprietors of the playhouse. By May 11, 1612, however, he describes himself as a Stratford resident in a London lawsuit – an indication that he had withdrawn from day-to-day professional activity and returned to the town where he had always had his main financial interests. When Shakespeare bought a substantial residential building in London, the Blackfriars Gatehouse, close to the theater of the same name, on March 10, 1613, he is recorded as William Shakespeare "of Stratford upon Avon in the county of Warwick, gentleman," and he named several London residents as the building's trustees. Still, he continued to participate in theatrical activity: when the new Earl of Rutland needed an allegorical design to bear as a shield, or *impresa*, at the celebration of King James's Accession Day, March 24, 1613, the earl's accountant recorded a payment of 44 shillings to Shakespeare for the device with its motto.

For the last few years of his life, Shakespeare evidently concentrated his activities in the town of his birth. Most of the final records concern business transactions in Stratford, ending with the notation of his death on April 23, 1616, and burial in Holy Trinity Church, Stratford-upon-Avon.

THE QUESTION OF AUTHORSHIP

The history of ascribing Shakespeare's plays (the poems do not come up so often) to someone else began, as it continues, peculiarly. The earliest published claim that someone else wrote Shakespeare's plays appeared in an 1856 article by Delia Bacon in the American journal *Putnam's Monthly* – although an Englishman, Thomas Wilmot, had shared his doubts in private (even secretive) conversations with friends near the end of the eighteenth century. Bacon's was a sad personal history that ended in madness and poverty, but the year after her article, she published, with great difficulty and the bemused assistance of Nathaniel Hawthorne (then United States Consul in Liverpool, England), her *Philosophy of the Plays of Shakspere Unfolded*. This huge, ornately written, confusing farrago is almost unreadable; sometimes its intents, to say nothing of its arguments, disappear entirely beneath near-raving, ecstatic writing. Tumbled in with much supposed "philosophy" appear the claims that Francis Bacon (from whom Delia Bacon eventually claimed descent), Walter Ralegh, and several other contemporaries of

Shakespeare's had written the plays. The book had little impact except as a ridiculed curiosity.

Once proposed, however, the issue gained momentum among people whose conviction was the greater in proportion to their ignorance of sixteenth- and seventeenth-century English literature, history, and society. Another American amateur, Catherine P. Ashmead Windle, made the next influential contribution to the cause when she published *Report to the British Museum* (1882), wherein she promised to open "the Cipher of Francis Bacon," though what she mostly offers, in the words of S. Schoenbaum, is "demented allegorizing." An entire new cottage industry grew from Windle's suggestion that the texts contain hidden, cryptographically discoverable ciphers — "clues" — to their authorship; and today there are not only books devoted to the putative ciphers, but also pamphlets, journals, and newsletters.

Although Baconians have led the pack of those seeking a substitute Shakespeare, in *"Shakespeare" Identified* (1920), J. Thomas Looney became the first published "Oxfordian" when he proposed Edward de Vere, seventeenth earl of Oxford, as the secret author of Shakespeare's plays. Also for Oxford and his "authorship" there are today dedicated societies, articles, journals, and books. Less popular candidates — Queen Elizabeth and Christopher Marlowe among them — have had adherents, but the movement seems to have divided into two main contending factions, Baconian and Oxfordian. (For further details on all the candidates for "Shakespeare," see S. Schoenbaum, *Shakespeare's Lives,* 2nd ed., 1991.)

The Baconians, the Oxfordians, and supporters of other candidates have one trait in common — they are snobs. Every pro-Bacon or pro-Oxford tract sooner or later claims that the historical William Shakespeare of Stratford-upon-Avon could not have written the plays because he could not have had the training, the university education, the experience, and indeed the imagination or background their author supposedly possessed. Only a learned genius like Bacon or an aristocrat like Oxford could have written such fine plays. (As it happens, lucky male children of the middle class had access to better education than most aristocrats in Elizabethan England – and Oxford was not particularly well educated.) Shakespeare received in the Stratford grammar school a formal education that would daunt many college graduates today; and popular rival playwrights such as the very learned Ben Jonson and George Chapman, both of whom also lacked university training, achieved great artistic success, without being taken as Bacon or Oxford.

Besides snobbery, one other quality characterizes the authorship controversy: lack of evidence. A great deal of testimony from Shakespeare's time shows that Shakespeare wrote Shakespeare's plays and that his contemporaries recognized them as distinctive and distinctly superior. (Some of that contemporary evidence is collected in E. K. Chambers, *William Shakespeare: A Study of Facts and Problems,* 2 vols., 1930.) Since that testimony comes from Shakespeare's enemies and theatrical competitors as well as from his co-workers and from the Elizabethan equivalent of literary journalists, it seems unlikely that, if any of these sources had known he was a fraud, they would have failed to record that fact.

Books About Shakespeare's Life

The following books provide scholarly, documented accounts of Shakespeare's life: G. E. Bentley, *Shakespeare: A Biographical Handbook* (1961); E. K. Chambers, *William Shakespeare: A Study of Facts and Problems,* 2 vols. (1930); S. Schoenbaum, *William Shakespeare: A Compact Documentary Life* (1977); and *Shakespeare's Lives,* 2nd ed. (1991), by the same author. Many scholarly editions of Shakespeare's complete works print brief compilations of essential dates and events. References to Shakespeare's works up to 1700 are collected in C. M. Ingleby et al., *The Shakespeare Allusion-Book*, rev. ed., 2 vols. (1932).

THE TEXTS OF SHAKESPEARE

As far as we know, only one manuscript conceivably in Shakespeare's own hand may (and even this is much disputed) exist: a few pages of a play called *Sir Thomas More*, which apparently was never performed. What we do have, as later readers, performers, scholars, students, are printed texts. The earliest of these survive in two forms: quartos and folios. Quartos (from the Latin for "four") are small books, printed on sheets of paper that were then folded in fours, to make eight double-sided pages. When these were bound together, the result was a squarish, eminently portable volume that sold for the relatively small sum of sixpence (translating in modern terms to about $5.00). This is the format in which Shakespeare's sonnets and narrative poems were printed. In folios, on the other hand, the sheets are folded only once, in half, producing large, impressive volumes taller than they are wide. This was the format for important works of philosophy, science, theology, and literature (the major precedent for a folio Shakespeare was Ben Jonson's *Works*, 1616). The decision to print the works of a popular playwright in folio is an indication of how far up on the social scale the theatrical profession had come during Shakespeare's lifetime. The Shakespeare folio was an expensive book, selling for between fifteen and eighteen shillings, depending on the binding (in modern terms, from about $150 to $180). Twenty Shakespeare plays of the thirty-seven that survive first appeared in quarto, seventeen of which appeared during Shakespeare's lifetime; the rest of the plays are found only in folio.

The First Folio was published in 1623, seven years after Shakespeare's death, and was authorized by his fellow actors, the co-owners of the King's Men. This publication was certainly a mark of the company's enormous respect for Shakespeare; but it was also a way of turning the old plays, most of which were no longer current in the playhouse, into ready money (the folio includes only Shakespeare's plays, not his sonnets or other nondramatic verse). Whatever the motives behind the publication of the folio, the texts it preserves constitute the basis for almost all later editions of the playwright's works. The texts, however, differ from those of the earlier quartos, sometimes in minor respects but often significantly – most strikingly in the two texts of *King Lear,* but also in important ways in *Hamlet, Othello,* and *Troilus and Cressida.* (The variants are recorded in the textual notes to each play in the new Pelican series.) The differences in these texts represent, in a sense, the essence of theater: the texts of plays were initially not intended for publication. They were scripts, designed for the actors to perform – the principal life of the play at this period was in performance. And it follows that in Shakespeare's theater the playwright typically had no say either in how his play was performed or in the disposition of his text – he was an employee of the company. The authoritative figures in the theatrical enterprise were the shareholders in the company, who were for the most part the major actors. They decided what plays were to be done; they hired the playwright and often gave him an outline of the play they wanted him to write. Often, too, the play was a collaboration: the company would retain a group of writers, and parcel out the scenes among them. The resulting script was then the property of the company, and the actors would revise it as they saw fit during the course of putting it on stage. The resulting text belonged to the company. The playwright had no rights in it once he had been paid. (This system survives largely intact in the movie industry, and most of the playwrights of Shakespeare's time were as anonymous as most screenwriters are today.) The script could also, of course, continue to change as the tastes of audiences and the requirements of the actors changed. Many – perhaps most – plays were revised when they were reintroduced after any substantial absence from the repertory, or when they were performed by a company different from the one that originally commissioned the play.

Shakespeare was an exceptional figure in this world because he was not only a shareholder and actor in his company, but also its leading playwright – he was literally his own boss. He had, moreover, little interest in the publication of his plays, and even those that appeared during his lifetime with the authorization of the company show no signs of any editorial concern on the part of the author. Theater was, for Shakespeare, a fluid and supremely responsive medium – the very opposite of the great classic canonical text that has embodied his works since 1623.

The very fluidity of the original texts, however, has meant that Shakespeare has always had to be edited. Here is an example of how problematic the editorial project inevitably is, a passage from the most famous speech in *Romeo and Juliet,* Juliet's balcony soliloquy beginning "O Romeo, Romeo, wherefore art thou Romeo?" Since the eighteenth century, the standard modern text has read,

> What's Montague? It is nor hand, nor foot,
> Nor arm, nor face, nor any other part
> Belonging to a man. O be some other name!
> What's in a name? That which we call a rose
> By any other name would smell as sweet.
>
> (II.2.40–44)

Editors have three early texts of this play to work from, two quarto texts and the folio. Here is how the First Quarto (1597) reads:

> Whats *Mountague?* It is nor band nor foote,
> Nor arme, nor face, nor any other part.
> Whats in a name? That which we call a Rofe,
> By any other name would fmell as fweet:

Here is the Second Quarto (1599):

> Whats *Mountague?* it is nor hand nor foote,
> Nor arme nor face, ô be fome other name
> Belonging to a man.
> Whats in a name that which we call a rofe,
> By any other word would fmell as fweete,

And here is the First Folio (1623):

> What's *Mountague?* it is nor hand nor foote,
> Nor arme, nor face, O be fome other name
> Belonging to a man.
> What? in a names that which we call a Rofe,
> By any other word would fmell as fweete,

There is in fact no early text that reads as our modern text does – and this is the most famous speech in the play. Instead, we have three quite different texts, all of which are clearly some version of the same speech, but none of which seems to us a final or satisfactory version. The transcendently beautiful passage in modern editions is an editorial invention: editors have succeeded in conflating and revising the three versions into something we recognize as great poetry. Is this what Shakespeare "really" wrote? Who can say? What we can say is that Shakespeare always had performance, not a book, in mind.

Books About the Shakespeare Texts

The standard study of the printing history of the First Folio is W. W. Greg, *The Shakespeare First Folio* (1955). J. K. Walton, *The Quarto Copy for the First Folio of Shakespeare* (1971), is a useful survey of the relation of the quartos to the folio. The second edition of Charlton Hinman's *Norton Facsimile* of the First Folio (1996), with a new introduction by Peter Blayney, is indispensable. Stanley Wells, Gary Taylor, John Jowett, and William Montgomery, *William Shakespeare: A Textual Companion,* keyed to the Oxford text, gives a comprehensive survey of the editorial situation for all the plays and poems.

THE GENERAL EDITORS

Introduction

IN THE WINTER of 1609 a seventeen-year-old Cambridge undergraduate sent two sonnets to his mother as a New Year's gift. They were addressed to God. The first one asked "doth poetry / Wear Venus' livery, only serve her turn? / Why are not sonnets made of thee? and lays / Upon thine altar burnt?" The second one, answering it, expressed the resolve of the young poet (it was George Herbert) to retune his poetic instrument to a sacred mode. That year was not a particularly fashionable one for sonnets. The vogue of sonnet sequences written in the wake of Sir Philip Sidney's remarkable *Astrophil and Stella*, written in the earlier 1580s but first published posthumously in 1591, was already a thing of the past. But 1609 also saw the publication of the sonnets of William Shakespeare, a most problematic book containing some of the greatest short lyric poems in our language. Herbert might have been sympathetic to the concerns of only one of the whole collection, "Poor soul, the center of my sinful earth," Sonnet 146, with its closing paradox ("And Death once dead, there's no more dying then"), similar to that at the end of John Donne's Holy Sonnet "Death be not proud" ("Death, thou shalt die"). But even in Shakespeare's poem the speaker never appeals to God for assistance or counsel, and addresses the appeal to his own soul – the poem is charged with autonomy, in the way in which it speaks for a mind with cognitive power over both the soul and the body of the person it shares with them.

"With this key," says a sonnet of Wordsworth's, "Shakespeare unlocked his heart." "Key" here means sonnet as form and mode. It is true that the "I" of these poems is unique in not being identified with a dramatic character in a play – in short, that these are Shakespeare's lyric poems. But if what is meant is that he recorded events in his life and his feelings about them as in a diary – even an enciphered one – then that is a different matter. We would have to conclude that what in fact he unlocked was a cabinet containing a coffer with its own lock whose combination no one has been able to discover. (And thus leaving us, too, with the possibility that it isn't really a combination lock at all, but a dummy set into a door that had been welded shut by circumstance.)

It cannot be denied that in and by many of these poems Shakespeare is telling a story about love and friendship, and the relation of time and poetry to these. (This story is also true in the "slant" way that Emily Dickinson urged poetry to talk.) But Shakespeare is also exploring the rhetorical and logical spaces of the interior of the sonnet form he favors – the three-quatrain-and-couplet pattern previously used exclusively by Samuel Daniel in his *Delia* (1592). The collection also varies certain of the relations that may develop among individual sonnets. These may exhibit a close sequential connection, as with numbers 64-65, or, even more, of 67-68, which read like two stanzas of a longer poem (they both speak, as well, of a "he" with no "you" or "thou" addressed), or yet again with Sonnets 50 and 51. And there it is additionally instructive to contrast their conceit of riding horseback with analogous ones in Sidney's *Astrophil and Stella* numbers 41, 49, and 84, with their underlying pun on the poet's Christian name, Philip (*phil-hippos,* or horse lover), and perhaps even with John Donne's later "Good Friday, 1613: Riding Westward." Or they may be completely independent poems, almost solitary on their page and in no way companioned by anything on a facing or following one. And yet the sonnets as a whole are a great puzzle, and it is equally true that with the key of the sonnet Shakespeare unlocked a chest – in a pun (on body part and inanimate coffer) that he himself uses in Sonnets 48 and 52 – full of enigmas of various sorts.

These enigmas seem to be nested one inside another. First, there are the troublesome matters of just what sort of book we are addressing. The quarto volume entitled *Shake-speares Sonnets. Never before Imprinted* that appeared in 1609 is itself something of an enigma. At least two of these sonnets had indeed been "before Imprinted" ten years earlier. It is famously and enigmatically dedicated by "T. T." (presumably the book's publisher, Thomas Thorpe) to "The Only Begetter of these ensuing Sonnets, Mr. W. H." And the dedication is itself puzzling – does Only Begetter mean sole, or incomparable, inspirer (or less probably, procurer for publication of the manuscript)? Mr. W. H. has been variously and inconclusively identified as, among others, the Earls of Southampton or Pembroke, someone or other named William Hughes, or even (most implausibly, and with a sense of begetter meaning creator) "William Himself." The syntax of the dedication is ambiguous (is "W. H." or "T. T." the subject of "wisheth" in the dedication's "wisheth the well-wishing adventurer in setting forth"?). But this is merely an overture to all the other enigmas: how "begotten" in any meaning of the term? How collected and/or selected, then how constructed and arranged? And by whom? What was Shakespeare's role in the publication of the book? Was it done with his approval? At his encouragement? Against his will? To his distress?

Then again, what *sort* of book is this: what is its genre? It is by no means purely a traditional sonnet sequence. Prior sonnet sequences are addressed to a central passive agent, a female figure both Muse and contingent erotic object. The convention runs through Beatrice, in Dante's *La Vita Nuova*, to Petrarch's Laura in the long sequence that replaces Dante's prose narrative and commentaries with more sonnets, and thereafter to Sir Philip Sidney's Stella, Samuel Daniel's Delia, and Michael Drayton's

Idea, among others. The full sonnet sequence would work through an array of situations and stances involving Sonneteer and Lady; they would work and play, within particular sonnets, with an ever wider array of poetic tropes in their discourse, very often with the sort of series of detailed and concrete metaphors or similes called "conceits." But this book seems to contain parts of at least two sequences, both problematic, addressed to a Young Man and the so-called Dark Lady – the "woman colored ill" (Sonnet 144) – as well as some vagrant sonnets, one (145) anomalous in being in tetrameters, and vastly inferior to the others, another (126) with only twelve lines, another (99) with fifteen, and two, included at the end of the book, in a totally different poetic mode. In a number of respects they seemingly fly in the face of the tradition of sonneteering: (1) the central personages are unnamed, as if to launder them of allegorical fictiveness, and *seemingly* to suggest thereby that they are unnamed actual persons; (2) the longest sequence is to a young man, not a woman; (3) the man and the woman both betray the poet by sleeping together; (4) a rival poet appears in Sonnet 78 and thereafter, surfacing most prominently in 86. An additional complication is that various poems, even some about love for the Young Man or the Lady, may actually be addressed to: Time (123); love itself, whether as Cupid or more abstractly personified (56, 126, 137, 148); the speaker's own soul (146); nobody, as soliloquies or asides or meditations (63, 64, 66, 67, 68, 94, 116, 119, 121, 124, 127, 129, 130, 138, 144, 153, 154); or nobody until the couplet (60, 62, 107, 118).

Finally, (5) the matter of moral and even metaphysical realms separating the somewhat heavenly Lady and the devoted but imperfect Sonneteer of the whole prior tradition (Spenser's sonnets being an exception, as they are all to a fiancée whom he will marry by the end of the sequence) is supplanted by what seems to be a relation of aristocrat/bourgeois – indeed, as C. L. Barber and

William Empson have both put it, there is something of Prince Hal/Falstaff here. But the Young Man, like the Ladies of the sequences, is mute. Moreover, only rarely, as in Sonnets 2 or 32, does the Poet make up actual words the Young Man might have uttered. We may wonder if all these anomalies make the Young Man more or less of a functioning agent than the more usual sonnet ladies: more, perhaps, because of gender and status, but perhaps less within the dialectic of any single poem. Then, too, the replacement of the ideal ladies of the standard sequences with an unnamed young man who is urged in sixteen of the first seventeen sonnets to marry and produce heirs resonates even more interestingly in an Elizabethan atmosphere. Italian Renaissance poets living in city-states ruled by powerful princes can indeed be thought of as seeking another kind of power in and from an imaginary realm ruled by a muselike mistress. But in 1590s England, the ruler was an extremely powerful woman, and there had indeed been concern, in the earlier part of her reign, that she produce an heir to the throne for stabilization as well as for continuity of a Protestant monarchy. And yet, save for the queen and an occasional figure like the Countess of Pembroke, a poet herself, most of the dedicatory poems to larger works of the 1590s and after were addressed to male patrons. Framed in sonnet form, with an agenda of deference to power and wealth rather than with ones of eros and intellect, these poems often braided together strands of supplication and instruction. The sonnets addressing the Young Man seem to partake of this mode as well.

Aside from these and many other enigmas turning on *what* exactly the book called *Shake-speares Sonnets* is, there is a problematic *when?* as well. The quarto volume was published well after the vogue of the major sonnet sequences in the 1590s. Sonnets 138 ("When my love swears that she is made of truth") and 144 ("Two loves I have, of comfort and despair") had been published in a collection called *The Passionate Pilgrim* in 1599, presumably with Shakespeare's permission; it is easiest to guess that most of them were written during the 1590s. There are tantalizing possibilities of associating particular sonnets with particular Shakespearean plays: 121, "'Tis better to be vile than vile esteemed," sounds more like something written by the author of *Measure for Measure* (c. 1604) than by the writer of most of the poems coming earlier in the book. But even this is dicey, because there is no reason to assume that, if any of them were written during the composition of – or period of composition of – a particular play they would sound like it. There are sonnets embedded in some of the speeches in *Love's Labor's Lost* and *Romeo and Juliet*, but they do not particularly sound like those of *The Sonnets* that might well have been written concurrently. Certain of the poems have been used to try to fix dates for themselves and, by inference, the others. Sonnet 107, "Not mine own fears . . . ," is full of bait for historical decoders, with line 5, "The mortal moon hath her eclipse endured," being identified as everything from the Spanish armada (1588) through the queen's grand climacteric or illness and/or a lunar eclipse (1595) to the death of Elizabeth in 1603. In another instance, 123 insists "No, Time, thou shalt not boast that I do change: / Thy pyramids built up with newer might / To me are nothing novel, nothing strange," and some scholars have used these lines to try to date this poem with respect to some celebrated "obelisks" – taken literally – newly built or installed in London, whether in the late 1580s or in 1603. Without question, "newly built structures we can experience firsthand and that might look like or allude to ancient ones" are clearly meant: they are crucial to the point of the poem – namely, that time will ruin the very difference between past and present. But assuming that "obelisks" are not metonymic, and that specifically topical ones must be meant, by no means provides a terminus a quo for all the sonnets. In any event, the dates of composition of these poems remain as problematic as the other circumstances of their being written.

The most haunting problem has been, at least from the eighteenth century on, the matter of fact and fiction in these sonnets. The relation of these two terms is, for literature, itself problematic. In poetry, can a fiction be "true to" fact without literally reporting it? Of how much fact and how much fiction are complex fictions composed? And how much might Shakespeare have wanted to do with all levels and sorts of lyric conventions in these poems what he does with dramatic conventions in the plays (as perhaps Chaucer does with late medieval narrative conventions in the *Tales*)? From Petrarch's "Laura" on, sonnet Ladies had been enigmatically compounded, and writers can easily set up what Dante called in *La Vita Nuova "schermo della veritade"* – a screen for the truth – by doing just the opposite of what a literal-minded person might think: protecting a private muse dwelling in the spaces of one's imagination by putting it out that she is merely a coded version of one's Mistress.

But if literalists are to be accorded their wish that the sonnets' elusive "story" be factual, then one is faced with the who-what-when-where-how-why of reportage. Candidates for the Young Man (Pembroke, Southampton) require fictional filling-in of gaps in Shakespeare's biography. But then what of the historical substance of the immensely complex relationship invented in the poems? What of the components of eros and philia – are the Poet and the Young Man friends or lovers or both in some sequence? And when this has been decided, what about Shakespeare and (let's call him) "X"? The Shakespeare-X relationship can be truly, but not necessarily literally, represented by the Poet–Young Man one. Shakespeare must have been closely familiar with situations arising from a relationship of the Poet–Young Man sort; but to what degree can anything about these be deciphered from messages that, if in some sort of code, are probably enciphering all sorts of other things, as poetry is always doing? And the so-called Dark Lady has been claimed to be any number of actual women, from one of the queen's maids of honor, named Mary Fitton, to, more recently, Emilia Lanier, a poet herself. Oscar Wilde's fictional exposition in "The Portrait of Master W. H." propounded a notional but historical "master mistress" (20) of the poet's passion, a true Mr. W. H., in the person of one Willie Hughes, a boy actor (who, of course, would have played women's roles on the stage). Anthony Burgess's splendid novel *Nothing Like the Sun* develops an equally compelling historical personage whose representation is the Dark Lady. Each of these fictions has a very different "sonnet theory" ad hoc to its own, imaginative concerns, but of greater worth, we tend to feel, than some of the more glumly literal speculations of scholars. And as for the Rival Poet: must we identify him as, for example, George Chapman? Or can we think of an exemplary rival poetry, creeping up out of references to other people's writing and inferior conventional contemporary poetry, and personified in the whole story's strangely oblique quadrilateral of Poet–Young Man–Dark Lady–Rival Poet?

Serious readers of poetry today, whether professional scholars or not, would certainly stop short of the kind of near-paranoid cryptanalysis that used to be pursued by those who felt that they had been given the key to Shakespeare's "heart" rather than his art. (Robert Browning scorned this view, responding to "Shakespeare unlocked his heart" in the last line of his poem "House": "Did Shakespeare? If so, the less Shakespeare he!") Such readers seem to believe that lyric poetry can allude to nothing but autobiographical minutiae. For example, Sonnet 37 begins with a simile associated with the matter of progeny and the punning deployment of words like "husbandry" that arose in the first group of seventeen:

As a decrepit father takes delight
To see his active child do deeds of youth,
So I, made lame by fortune's dearest spite,
Take all my comfort of thy worth and truth.

("Dearest" could mean both "most dire" and "most costly" here.) It may be no surprise that pious literalists in the past devoted pages to conjecture about whether Shakespeare had been crippled by a birth defect, had suffered permanent injury by accident, say, or in battle, instead of realizing that the comparison in the second part of the simile propounded what was itself a metaphoric attribute. Speculations about other moments in *The Sonnets* may, indeed, seem more promising – e.g., whether in Sonnet 153's line 11 about how the speaker, "sick withal, the help of bath desired," refers to any spa or to the city of Bath in particular. And speculations about the Rival Poet are more interesting in that they engage some critical interpretation of the Poet's sense of the particular character of his own work. Chapman, mentioned previously, is the usual candidate: in Sonnet 86 "the proud full sail of his great verse, / Bound for the prize of all-too-precious you" could be the long fourteener of that poet's translation of the *Iliad*, and it is easy to imagine the line about "his compeers by night" alluding to Chapman's literary circle (as some lines in *Love's Labor's Lost* seem to do as well). Shakespeare did indeed unlock some of his art with the poetic turning of *The Sonnets* – we need only compare the best of them with the occasional sonnets embedded in the dialogue in *Love's Labor's Lost* or *Romeo and Juliet* – but *only thereby* did he perhaps open up some of his heart. For it is in a poet's art that his or her heart is to be found. Or to put it another way, any poet writing in the first person has more than one heart and two I's.

Yet even if the sonnets are all made of the whole cloth of fiction, other questions jostle for attention. What genre of sonnet fiction is it that puts a situation rather than a single passive female figure at its center? What kinds of "story" are unfolded or hinted at? What – and this is crucial – about the ordering of these poems? We certainly start out with the sense of a sequential run: Sonnets 1-126 all speak to the Young Man, 1-17 urging him to beget "breed, to brave him [Time] when he takes thee hence" (12). But before the end of this run comes Sonnet 15, with no mention of marriage and children, save for a possible associative substitution of poetic grafting for a natural line of descent. Unlike the others that precede it, opening with what could be the start of a speech of Richard II's, it is anomalous also in that it has "you" for "thou." Sonnets 127-152 concern the dark-haired woman, but no narrative emerges from their sequential ordering. Indeed, we cannot even be sure that, purely in fictional terms, the woman who betrays him with the friend in, say, 40 and 42 is the same dark-haired "woman colored ill" (144) of the later group. We do indeed find other sorts of short sequential runs, but there are many seemingly random interjections. Certainly interrupting a related run is the trivial and possibly even non-Shakespearean 145, followed by the very great 146 (almost as if in subsequent poetic self-rebuke. But only almost . . .). Thematic matters can suggest vague groupings, most often not acknowledged sequentially. Time and Love are part of the whole set's deepest structures, rather than "topics" of individual poems. The theme of the power of poetic representation to outlast its object runs throughout the sequence. Sonnets 71-74 concern the Poet's own death, and the autumnal 73 ("That time of year thou mayst in me behold") is perhaps no irrelevant intervention.

Mentioned earlier was the resolution manifested in Sonnet 146 (one of those seemingly out of the sequence in every way – it occurs toward the end of the Dark Lady series, following immediately upon the possibly spurious

145). An even stronger resolution of another sort pervades the magnificent 121:

'Tis better to be vile than vile esteemed
When not to be receives reproach of being,
And the just pleasure lost, which is so deemed
Not by our feeling but by others' seeing.
For why should others' false adulterate eyes
Give salutation to my sportive blood?
Or on my frailties why are frailer spies,
Which in their wills count bad what I think good?
No, I am that I am; and they that level
At my abuses reckon up their own:
I may be straight though they themselves be bevel;
By their rank thoughts my deeds must not be shown,
    Unless this general evil they maintain:
    All men are bad and in their badness reign.

– "I am what I am, not what your reproaches make me seem": this is also literally, with something close to blasphemy, God speaking out of the burning bush in Exodus 3:14, refusing to give Moses his name or otherwise account for himself.

There seems to be almost no sequential connection between this poem and those surrounding it. Sonnet 122, the following one, is related to the commonplace book conceit in 77, the reciprocal gifts of blank books clearly associating them. It seems more fruitful to consider the preceding group: 117, full of self-rebuke; then 118, a tough-minded assessment bringing images of illness, satiation, purges, and drugs to matters of "policy in love." This is again followed by more self-rebuke of a different sort that opens 119: "What potions have I drunk of siren tears / Distilled from limbecks foul as hell within. . . ." The sonnet eventually turns that rebuke around by perceiving "That better is by evil still made better"; but this still leaves some readers with the puzzle of whether the "siren tears" – expressions luring men to moral shipwreck – are those of the Dark Lady who appears eight sonnets later, or of some other women, or more general and unspecified traps. Similarly, in Sonnet 120, which broods over reciprocal unkindnesses, "our night of woe" could be taken both as a single night in which unkindnesses or even unnaturalnesses might have occurred or, more metaphorically, a period of time in the lives of both. But in any case, the mode and the tone and the argument do not suggest that the intended addressee is the Young Man, who is never exposed to such a strongly direct and unabashed self-defense of the Poet.

Even without direct sequentiality, our own critical consciousness may want to group sonnets thematically, but the poems themselves too often resist this. "Shall I compare thee to a summer's day?" (18) and the very great "That time of year thou mayst in me behold" (73) are not really a summer/autumn diptych, and their central tropes are framed quite differently (*let's see how you're nicer even than summer* vs. *"in" me are autumn, sundown twilight, dying embers),* which is more to the point.

Similarly in the case of two of the minor sonnets spinning out musical conceits: Sonnet 8, addressed to the Young Man, is about love as harmony – it starts out in the tone of Lorenzo replying to Jessica in Act V, scene 1 of *The Merchant of Venice,* when she says "I am never merry when I hear sweet [i.e., well-tuned] music" (l. 69), but with a totally different response. The different "parts" of polyphonic musical composition rebuke the "singleness" of the Young Man's refusal to marry. The sonnet pivots at the end of the eighth line – ". . . the parts that thou shouldst bear" – and moves toward actualities as well as tropes of bearing children. The figure is of sympathetic vibration observed in two strings tuned in exact unison, one of which when struck will cause the other to sound, but here more precisely suggesting paired lute strings.

> Mark how one string, sweet husband to another,
> Strikes each in each by mutual ordering;
> Resembling sire and child and happy mother,
> Who, all in one, one pleasing note do sing;
>   Whose speechless song, being many, seeming one,
>   Sings this to thee, "Thou single wilt prove none."

Fruitful musical unison born of union rebukes bachelorhood as a single note sings against the single state. But in the more trivial musical Sonnet 128, to the Lady, "How oft, when thou, my music, music play'st" – which might be part of a speech from an early comedy – the Lady is seen playing the virginal. The keys (miscalled "jacks," which are in fact the small blocks that pluck the strings) are envied because they "kiss the tender inward" of her hand as she plays, "Making dead wood more blessed than living lips"; this is followed by the injunction to let the Poet do the literal kissing. Both these poems might be thought of as occasional, but the occasions are of two different sorts. In the second, a narrative vignette proposes itself, and the writer asks himself, *what can I do with a lady-at-the-spinet bit?* In the case of the first, the occasion is conceptual: *given the "beget children" agenda I'm working with, what can be done with "bear musical part" and "bear offspring," and with "single vs. unified"?* In *The Sonnets* there are many different sorts of occasions for particular poems. These range from variations of posture, praise, blame, and their interrelations, representations of various sorts, themes and topics, previous turns on particular words or conceits, and many others.

But there are some turns Shakespeare does not take. For example: Sidney, in *Astrophil and Stella* 71, uses a celebrated device of giving pure pattern a figurative significance. In a poem praising "Stella"'s power in helping the poet sublimate his libido, he concludes:

> So while thy beauty draws the heart to love,
> As fast thy virtue bends that love to good:
> But ah, Desire still cries, give me some food.

This is a sonnet whose scheme, like Shakespeare's, is 4+4+4+2, but notice how the couplet is broken: "love" and "good" don't rhyme, but the lines ending in them seem to form a couplet, while there is a strong gap between those actually rhyming "good" and "food." A contemporary poem might drop the last line down three spaces to jab home the point (that love will find out the way, even here). One feels that, for Sidney, trying out this pattern seems itself to be an occasion. For Shakespeare, it is words that present multiple meanings to play on, and patterns of thought inviting dialectical formulations, that provide analogous occasions for particular sonnets.

If the nineteenth century cared to dwell most on biographical mysteries in *The Sonnets*, our own time would be most concerned with the thematically general question of representation itself – it has been in the last half century that we characteristically translate the central Greek word "mimesis" as "representation" rather than, as previously, "imitation," and for lyric poetry, the term covers both an "imitation" and "expression," so insistently differentiated by earlier critics. Tropes of representation abound in the sonnets, and they interanimate each other as most of the other occasional conceits (the wonderful one of the law court with the strong benign judge in Sonnet 30, for example) do not. They include: shadows (e.g., in 43 and 53); portraiture (24, 68); painting as facial makeup (20, 21, 83); acting and theater (23); mirrors (3, 22, 77); dreams (43, 61); writing (38, 76, 78-82, 84-86, 100-101, 106).

These images point up deep enigmas of the poems'

own fictiveness, and focus a reader's attention on a modern rather than on a more romantic agenda. The art of *The Sonnets* is liberatingly – rather than cripplingly – self-conscious. The poems make shifting and often playfully contradictory claims for the authenticity of mortal persons and relations and feelings over mere but enduring writing about them. Often, when they say one thing about writing, they seem to mean another. For example, in Sonnet 32 the Young Man says of notional better poets' work (in the event that the Poet dies young), "Theirs for their style I'll read, his [the Poet's] for his love." But for a true poet, do not *style* and *love* themselves embrace? And isn't the distinction between them – a cloven fiction, William Blake would have called it – only there in bad poetry? "The truest poetry," we are reminded by Touchstone in *As You Like It*, may be "the most feigning" (III.3.17-18).

Again in the later-twentieth-century fashion, though, we may think also of repeatedly explored images as themes. "Eye" – whether punning, as it frequently does, on "I" or not – emerges potently in Sonnet 1. "But thou, contracted to thine own bright eyes" – whether or not implying that they are barren idols for the young man's attachment and engagement – plays so perilously close to the celestial territory of Sidney's cynosure Stella that it is hard to resist feeling there is some conscious adaptation of the original Petrarchan eyes here. From the key trope of the eye that opens the sequence to the "perjured eye/I" of Sonnet 152, the eyes have it for so much of this poetry. In 46-47, eye and heart become involved, and this relation gets worked through later on, even to the conventional matter of Cupid's blindness. "Husbandry" and the notion of possession are similarly both explored through their multiple meanings in many of the sonnets. But the Poet's "my" as well as his "I" are as fictive and as variously constructed in different poems as his "eye."

The very powerful and often difficult language of

The Sonnets thus becomes another problematic matter. If the Young Man possesses wealth, status, and beauty that the Poet does not, the poetic language denied both the Young Man and the Lady has a power beyond theirs. The Poet is himself a "master mistress" of what is syntactically very dense, often in collaboration with words that have complex senses. Ambiguities of punctuation, such as those confronted by the celebrated editorial re-pointings of Sonnet 129 ("Th' expense of spirit in a waste of shame"), abound. Fluidities of syntactic structures in poetic lines are basic to much late Elizabethan poetry: subject-verb-object order alternates with inversions of these, adjectives are used adverbially, etc. In *The Sonnets* Shakespeare uses most ambiguities functionally: for example, the line in Sonnet 64 about church monuments being defaced – "And brass eternal slave to mortal rage" – has eternal brass slave to mortal rage and brass being that slave eternally. Again, in "Love's not time's fool, though rosy lips and cheeks / Within his bending sickle's compass come" (116), "bending" means both "bent" and "causing to bend" – both true of sickles – and, along with the strong alliterative sequence *(sickle > compass > come)*, makes the clause ever more vivid. The poems abound with plainly effective kinds of syntactic play, such as the ubiquitous Elizabethan chiasm (or pattern within a line or two of *abba,* whether of sounds or parts of speech or concrete vs. abstract terms, etc.). This can be seen in the noun-adjective/adjective-noun line quoted above: *brass-eternal /mortal-rage,* and where *mortal* and *eternal* are opposed, while coexisting with another sense of *mortal* meaning "deadly." This kind of density gives the language of the sonnets its power, as do all the modes of wordplay, from the subtle, quiet, double senses of *mortal* just mentioned, to more flagrantly deployed erotic double meanings. There are even such patterns of assonance, as in the final line of Sonnet 38, "The pain be mine, but thine shall be the praise," where the arduous work of writing, when worked through the sequence of the chiasm *pain mine thine praise* (noun pronoun pronoun noun, /ey/ /ay/ /ay/ /ey/), emerges in and as "praise." And notice how for the next sonnet, 39, this last "praise" is like a bell to toll the speaker back to some of the questions that lie at the root of a poet's praise of someone else – by making the praise real poetry, isn't the maker thereof eliciting what he bestows? And with "What can mine own praise to mine own self bring" this issue is acknowledged. Effects like these – the chiasm, the picking up of words and images from previous sonnets and revising or expanding their functions – are frequent, and they are so beautifully worked that they seem to hide in the sense of the line they are invisibly deepening.

Linguistic puzzles in *The Sonnets* reach down even to the smallest level of a *thou/you* alternation. There are traces of sequence in these: Sonnet 13 is the first poem to address the Young Man as *you*, with its plays on *you/yourself*, etc.; then 15; 16; and Sonnets 52-55; 57-59; 71-72; 83-86; 106; 115; 118, and so forth. In the *you* Sonnets 83-86 a tone may be discerned that shifts sharply in 87 ("Farewell, thou art too dear for my possessing").

But here, again, there are moves in the game of words that are not played. In Sonnet 15, if Shakespeare were Milton, we might remark on one resonance of the verb in the opening line: "When I consider everything that grows" (*sider* = Latin "constellation"), in view of the image of the stars and their "influence" in lines 4-7. But Shakespeare's concern is not ordinarily to make the reader conscious of etymology – as if he cared himself, which he seems not to do most of the time. The history of words is not present for him, but the way they behave when thrust onstage with each other is central. Even in something as simple as "And beauty making beautiful old rhyme" (106), the question arises whether beauty is beautifying old rhyme, or whether what it makes is "beautiful old rhyme" to begin with. Such double turns are everywhere, and very often the force of the phrase, its compact and pointed power, depends on our consciousness of both such meanings without fear of having to promote one over another. The process of revelation that comes so often in *Paradise Lost*, the sense that one had misread first and has now to replace the older reading (usually this is done by an enjambment) is alien to this poetry, which is so much a collection – sometimes looking like a series, sometimes not – of moments of address, and of stock-taking, and brokering.

Generally, then, the unusual tightness and condensation of the language force ambiguous constructions of the sense of its sentences, which function themselves as signal rather than noise, as representations of an ambivalence in some ways more profound than any erotic or social or moral one. In his Ovidian narrative poem, *Venus and Adonis* (published in 1593, and dedicated to Southampton), Shakespeare seems to feel more like the young, erotically passive hunter Adonis, devoted less to the attentions of Venus than to his pursuit of venison; on the other hand, Venus's speeches, which occupy so much of the poem, have clearly been written with unrestrained gusto by – and in some ways, for – the poet himself as well. In *The Sonnets*, there is a sense of ambivalence in speaking as a sonnet writer at all, at having to speak in a first person as various and complex as, say, Walt Whitman's. After his earliest apprenticeship, one mark of Shakespeare's genius is shown in play after play as he takes a conventional or even fashionable theatrical subgenre or mode or plot and changes it reflexively, in a way that raises implicit questions about the nature and substance of the convention to begin with. There is no reason to suppose that in *The Sonnets* this deep inventiveness has been shelved, whether or not the enigmatic book we have consists of residues of abandoned attempts to write a Shakespearean sonnet sequence.

Finally, textual questions complicate linguistic ones.

Even though, given all the other enigmas, the text here is less of a problem than in the case of many of the plays, many emendations are obviously necessary, as in the case of Sonnet 146, in which the opening of the second line, "My sinful earth," impossibly repeats the last three words of the first. Problems of punctuation mentioned earlier abound. The 1609 quarto gives Sonnet 135, line 13 as "Let no unkind, no fair beseechers kill." This can simply urge both unkind and fair people not to kill those who implore them, or it can enjoin the unkind not to kill fair beseechers. But the word "no" might be the agent: following an emendation by Edmond Malone in the eighteenth century, we might parse the line as "Let no unkind 'No' fair beseechers kill," or "Let 'No,' unkind, no fair beseechers kill," or even "Let 'No,' unkind 'No,' fair beseechers kill," which totally reverses the sense and may be all but impossible. (It would be amusing to discover exactly which edition of *The Sonnets* Wallace Stevens had remembered this line from, given that it seems to return in "There is not nothing, no, no, never nothing, / Like the clashed edges of two words that kill" from "Le Monocle de Mon Oncle.")

But in the end it is not that we are put off by all these enigmas, made impatient by how much about these poems will seem ever to be left up for grabs. It is rather that there is so very much poetic stuff there. The question that opens the great Sonnet 53 – "What is your substance, whereof are you made, / That millions of strange shadows on you tend?" – is asked of the Young Man: what is it in him that attracts so many representations, images, fictions of and about him? But we may ask it as well, with respect to the myriads of kinds and instances of interpretation that hang about it, keep crowding toward it, of the book called *Shake-speares Sonnets*. Answering for ourselves that we can never know the substance is only an easy and vulgar pseudo-pragmatic escape if it causes us to abandon rereading and rethinking the vast question as well as the minute particulars of this remarkable poetry. A genuinely Keatsian negative capability does not stultify, but rather prevents intellectual paralysis.

In 1630 the young John Milton, having bought a copy of the Italian poet Giovanni della Casa's sonnets the year before, and having perhaps experimented with writing sonnets in Italian, in that revisionary mode composed his first sonnet to the nightingale in an appropriately Italian convention. It asked whether the song of the bird was a call to love or to poetry for the young virginal poet hearing it, as if heralding one or another of two modes of life that the Petrarchan sonnet tradition had brought metaphorically together. Perhaps he lacked sufficient experience, as well as temperament, to have learned that between Love and Poetry there is no either/or relation, but rather one, which Shakespeare's sonnets explore, of mutual and living begetting.

JOHN HOLLANDER
Yale University

Note on the Text

THE ONLY AUTHORITY for the text of the sonnets other than 138 and 144, versions of which had appeared in a volume of miscellaneous poetry called *The Passionate Pilgrim* (1599), is the quarto issued by the publisher Thomas Thorpe in 1609 (referred to hereafter as Q). Q also includes, in addition to the sonnets, the narrative poem *A Lover's Complaint,* long considered spurious but now generally accepted as Shakespeare's – the poem appears in the new Pelican series volume *The Narrative Poems.* How Thorpe came by his text remains a mystery, not at all enlightened by the dedication he provided to "the only begetter of these ensuing sonnets"; but it is unlikely to have been a manuscript in Shakespeare's hand, and there is no reason to believe that Shakespeare was actively involved in its publication. There is also, however, no justification for regarding the book as in any way surreptitious: Thorpe was not a piratical publisher. In 1640 John Benson issued a pirated edition of the sonnets, much rearranged and revised; this volume, however, has no independent authority and is textually of no value.

The present edition follows the text of Q. The following list of emendations is complete except for corrections of obvious misprints; the adopted reading is given in italics followed by the quarto reading in roman.

2: 4 *tattered* totter'd   12: 4 *o'ersilvered* or siluer'd; *are* ore   13: 7 *Your self* You selfe   25: 9 *fight* worth   26: 11 *tattered* tottered   26: 12 *thy* their   27: 10 *thy* their   31: 8 *thee* there   34: 12 *cross* losse   35: 8 *thy . . . thy* their . . . their   37: 7 *thy* their   39: 12 *doth* dost   43: 11 *thy* their   45: 12 *thy* their   46: 3, 8, 13, 14 *thy* their   47: 11 *not* nor   50: 6 *dully* duly   55: 1 *monuments* monument   65: 12 *of* or   69: 3 *due* end   69: 5 *Thy* Their   69: 14 *soil* solye   70: 1 *art* are   70: 6 *Thy* Their   76: 7 *tell* fel   77: 10 *blanks* blacks   99: 9 *One* Our   102: 8 *her* his   112: 14 *they're* y'are

113: 6 *latch* lack   113: 14 *mine eye* mine   126: 8 *minutes* mynuit   127: 10 *brows* eyes   128: 11 *thy* their   128: 14 *thy fingers* their fingers   129: 11 *proved, a* proud and   132: 6 *of the* of th'   132: 9 *mourning* morning   144: 6 *side* sight   146: 2 *Pressed by* My sinfull earth   153: 14 *eyes* eye

The Sonnets

TO THE ONLY BEGETTER OF
THESE ENSUING SONNETS
MR. W. H. ALL HAPPINESS
AND THAT ETERNITY
PROMISED
BY
OUR EVER-LIVING POET
WISHETH
THE WELL-WISHING
ADVENTURER IN
SETTING
FORTH
T.T.

The Sonnets

1

From fairest creatures we desire increase,   1
That thereby beauty's rose might never die,
But as the riper should by time decease,   3
His tender heir might bear his memory;   4
But thou, contracted to thine own bright eyes,   5
Feed'st thy light's flame with self-substantial fuel,   6
Making a famine where abundance lies,
Thyself thy foe, to thy sweet self too cruel.
Thou that art now the world's fresh ornament
And only herald to the gaudy spring,   10
Within thine own bud buriest thy content   11
And, tender churl, mak'st waste in niggarding.   12
   Pity the world, or else this glutton be,
   To eat the world's due, by the grave and thee.   14

---

1 *creatures* all living things (not just animals); *we . . . increase* (1) we wish for offspring, (2) we increase our desire **3** *riper* ripening, growing older **4** *tender* (as opposed to *riper*); *bear* carry on, preserve **5** *contracted to* betrothed only to (literally, bound by contract) **6** *self-substantial* self-consuming **10** *only* chief; *gaudy* luxuriant (not pejorative) **11** *bud* unopened flower (cf. *rose*, l. 2); *thy content* (1) what you contain (your potential offspring), (2) your satisfaction **12** *tender churl* (1) youthful miser, (2) sweet boor; *mak'st . . . niggarding* are wasteful in hoarding yourself **14** *To . . . thee* to swallow up, both by death and your own willfullness, what belongs to the world

2

When forty winters shall besiege thy brow
And dig deep trenches in thy beauty's field,
3 Thy youth's proud livery, so gazed on now,
4 Will be a tattered weed of small worth held:
Then being asked where all thy beauty lies,
6 Where all the treasure of thy lusty days,
To say within thine own deep-sunken eyes
8 Were an all-eating shame and thriftless praise.
9 How much more praise deserved thy beauty's use
10 If thou couldst answer, "This fair child of mine
11 Shall sum my count and make my old excuse,"
12 Proving his beauty by succession thine.
　　This were to be new made when thou art old
　　And see thy blood warm when thou feel'st it cold.

---

3 *proud livery* splendid display 4 *weed* garment 6 *lusty* passionate 8 *an all-eating* a devouring; *thriftless* unprofitable 9 *deserved* would deserve; *use* (1) sexual activity, (2) financial investment (cf. "usury") 11 *sum . . . count* settle my account; *make . . . excuse* justify my life when I am old 12 *succession* inheritance

3

Look in thy glass, and tell the face thou viewest
Now is the time that face should form another,
Whose fresh repair if now thou not renewest,   3
Thou dost beguile the world, unbless some mother.   4
For where is she so fair whose uneared womb   5
Disdains the tillage of thy husbandry?
Or who is he so fond will be the tomb   7
Of his self-love, to stop posterity?   8
Thou art thy mother's glass, and she in thee   9
Calls back the lovely April of her prime;   10
So thou through windows of thine age shalt see,   11
Despite of wrinkles, this thy golden time.
    But if thou live remembered not to be,   13
    Die single, and thine image dies with thee.

---

3 *fresh repair* youthful condition   4 *beguile* cheat; *unbless . . . mother* deprive
someone of the blessing of motherhood   5 *uneared* unplowed   7 *fond* fool-
ish 7–8 *be . . . self-love* entomb himself in self-love   8 *posterity* the perpetua-
tion of his line   9 *glass* mirror   11 *windows . . . age* i.e., the perspective
provided by old age   13 *remembered . . . be* only to be forgotten

4

Unthrifty loveliness, why dost thou spend
2 Upon thyself thy beauty's legacy?
Nature's bequest gives nothing but doth lend,
4 And, being frank, she lends to those are free.
5 Then, beauteous niggard, why dost thou abuse
The bounteous largesse given thee to give?
7 Profitless usurer, why dost thou use
8 So great a sum of sums, yet canst not live?
9 For, having traffic with thyself alone,
10 Thou of thyself thy sweet self dost deceive:
Then how, when nature calls thee to be gone,
What acceptable audit canst thou leave?
13   Thy unused beauty must be tombed with thee,
14   Which, usèd, lives th' executor to be.

---

2 *beauty's legacy* inheritance of beauty 4 *frank* bountiful; *are free* who are
generous (both financially and sexually) 5 *niggard* miser 7 *use* (1) use up,
(2) invest (without profit) 8 *live* (1) make a living, (2) survive (through off-
spring) 9 *traffic* dealings 10 *deceive* defraud 13 *unused* uninvested 14
lives i.e., in the person of a son (executors are male; hence, not a daughter,
despite the fact that in Sonnet 3 he himself is the image of his mother, not
his father)

5

Those hours that with gentle work did frame
The lovely gaze where every eye doth dwell   2
Will play the tyrants to the very same
And that unfair which fairly doth excel;   4
For never-resting time leads summer on
To hideous winter and confounds him there,   6
Sap checked with frost and lusty leaves quite gone,
Beauty o'ersnowed and bareness everywhere.
Then, were not summer's distillation left   9
A liquid prisoner pent in walls of glass,   10
Beauty's effect with beauty were bereft,   11
Nor it nor no remembrance what it was: 12
    But flowers distilled, though they with winter meet,
    Leese but their show; their substance still lives sweet.   14

---

2 *gaze* object of attention (the thing gazed on)   4 *unfair* deface; *fairly* (1) in beauty, (2) while still beautiful   6 *confounds* destroys   9 *distillation* essence (of flowers distilled into perfume)   11 *with . . . bereft* would be lost with the passing of beauty   12 *Nor it* (leaving behind) neither itself   14 *Leese* lose

6

1 Then let not winter's ragged hand deface
2 In thee thy summer ere thou be distilled:
3 Make sweet some vial; treasure thou some place
  With beauty's treasure ere it be self-killed.
5 That use is not forbidden usury
6 Which happies those that pay the willing loan;
7 That's for thyself to breed another thee,
8 Or ten times happier be it ten for one.
  Ten times thyself were happier than thou art,
10 If ten of thine ten times refigured thee:
  Then what could death do if thou shouldst depart,
  Leaving thee living in posterity?
    Be not self-willed, for thou art much too fair
    To be death's conquest and make worms thine heir.

---

1 *ragged* rough   2 *distilled* (see Sonnet 5, ll. 9 and 13)   3 *some vial* i.e., some woman's womb; *treasure* enrich   5 *forbidden usury* (lending money at interest had been legal since 1571, but was still considered morally reprehensible) 6 *happies* makes happy; *pay . . . loan* (1) repay the loan willingly offered, (2) willingly repay the loan (the syntax is "that use which makes those who willingly pay happy is not usury")   7 *That's* i.e., the purpose of that usury is   8 *ten for one* i.e., if you had ten children (suggesting the legal interest rate of 10 percent; though the rate here would be 1,000 percent)   10 *refigured* duplicated

7

Lo, in the orient when the gracious light   1
Lifts up his burning head, each under eye   2
Doth homage to his new-appearing sight,
Serving with looks his sacred majesty;
And having climbed the steep-up heavenly hill,   5
Resembling strong youth in his middle age,
Yet mortal looks adore his beauty still,
Attending on his golden pilgrimage;
But when from highmost pitch, with weary car,   9
Like feeble age he reeleth from the day,   10
The eyes, 'fore duteous, now converted are   11
From his low tract and look another way: 12
   So thou, thyself outgoing in thy noon,   13
   Unlooked on diest unless thou get a son.

---

1 *orient* east; *light* sun 2 *under* (1) earthly, (2) inferior (hence his subjects)
5 *steep-up* precipitous 9 *highmost pitch* the apex; *car* sun's chariot 11 *'fore*
previously; *converted* turned away 12 *tract* course 13 *outgoing . . . noon* (1)
surpassingly beautiful at your apex, (2) passing your prime

8

1 Music to hear, why hear'st thou music sadly?
  Sweets with sweets war not, joy delights in joy:
  Why lov'st thou that which thou receiv'st not gladly,
4 Or else receiv'st with pleasure thine annoy?
5 If the true concord of well-tunèd sounds,
6 By unions married, do offend thine ear,
7 They do but sweetly chide thee, who confounds
  In singleness the parts that thou shouldst bear.
  Mark how one string, sweet husband to another,
10 Strikes each in each by mutual ordering;
  Resembling sire and child and happy mother,
  Who, all in one, one pleasing note do sing;
      Whose speechless song, being many, seeming one,
14   Sings this to thee, "Thou single wilt prove none."

---

1 *Music to hear* you who are music to hear   4 *thine annoy* what troubles (or bores) you   5 *concord* harmony   6 *unions* (1) agreement of sounds (in polyphonic harmony), (2) wedlock   7–8 *confounds . . . bear* i.e., destroys the potential harmony (of marriage) by performing singly rather than in concert   10 *mutual ordering* sympathetic tuning (whereby two strings on a double-stringed lute, vibrating sympathetically, sound the same note when one is plucked)   14 *none* nothing, no one

9

Is it for fear to wet a widow's eye
That thou consum'st thyself in single life?
Ah, if thou issueless shalt hap to die,   3
The world will wail thee like a makeless wife;   4
The world will be thy widow, and still weep
That thou no form of thee hast left behind,
When every private widow well may keep,   7
By children's eyes, her husband's shape in mind.
Look what an unthrift in the world doth spend   9
Shifts but his place, for still the world enjoys it;   10
But beauty's waste hath in the world an end,
And, kept unused, the user so destroys it: 12
    No love toward others in that bosom sits
    That on himself such murd'rous shame commits.   14

---

3 *issueless* childless   4 *makeless* mateless   7 *private widow* (as opposed to *The world*, l. 4)   9 *Look what* consider that whatever; *an unthrift* a spendthrift   10 *his* its   12 *user* owner   14 *murd'rous shame* shameful murder

10

1 For shame deny that thou bear'st love to any
  Who for thyself art so unprovident:
3 Grant, if thou wilt, thou art beloved of many,
  But that thou none lov'st is most evident;
  For thou art so possessed with murd'rous hate
6 That 'gainst thyself thou stick'st not to conspire,
7 Seeking that beauteous roof to ruinate
8 Which to repair should be thy chief desire.
9 O, change thy thought, that I may change my mind.
10 Shall hate be fairer lodged than gentle love?
11 Be as thy presence is, gracious and kind,
  Or to thyself at least kindhearted prove:
    Make thee another self for love of me,
14   That beauty still may live in thine or thee.

---

1 *For . . . deny* (1) be ashamed of yourself and deny, (2) from a sense of shame deny   3 *Grant . . . wilt* granted, if you like   6 *thou . . . not* you do not scruple   7 *roof* house (both his body and his family); *ruinate* ruin   8 *repair* (1) keep in good repair, (2) restore   9 *thought* attitude; *change . . . mind* think differently of you   11 *presence* appearance   14 *still may* (1) may always, (2) may continue to

11

As fast as thou shalt wane so fast thou grow'st 1
In one of thine, from that which thou departest; 2
And that fresh blood which youngly thou bestow'st 3
Thou mayst call thine when thou from youth convertest. 4
Herein lives wisdom, beauty, and increase;
Without this, folly, age, and cold decay.
If all were minded so, the times should cease, 7
And threescore year would make the world away. 8
Let those whom Nature hath not made for store, 9
Harsh, featureless, and rude, barrenly perish: 10
Look whom she best endowed she gave the more, 11
Which bounteous gift thou shouldst in bounty cherish. 12
   She carved thee for her seal, and meant thereby 13
   Thou shouldst print more, not let that copy die. 14

1–2 *thou grow'st . . . thine* (1) you grow large in your wife (during sexual intercourse), (2) you continue to grow in your child   2 *from . . . departest* (1) as a result of what you send forth (in intercourse: *depart* is transitive, a stronger form of "impart"), (2) from the youth that you depart from   3 *youngly* (1) in youth, (2) energetically   4 *convertest* turn away   7 *times* generations   8 *threescore year* sixty years (less than the stipulated biblical term of human life, threescore and ten)   9 *for store* as breeding stock   10 *rude* crude   11 *Look . . . more* i.e., the most beautiful creatures have the greatest breeding capacity; *Look whom* whomever   12 *in bounty* by being similarly bountiful – i.e., prolific in breeding   13 *seal* stamp (with which to impress her image)   14 *copy* pattern (from which copies are made)

12

1 When I do count the clock that tells the time
2 And see the brave day sunk in hideous night,
When I behold the violet past prime
4 And sable curls o'ersilvered are with white,
When lofty trees I see barren of leaves,
6 Which erst from heat did canopy the herd,
7 And summer's green all girded up in sheaves
Borne on the bier with white and bristly beard;
9 Then of thy beauty do I question make
10 That thou among the wastes of time must go,
11 Since sweets and beauties do themselves forsake
And die as fast as they see others grow;
And nothing 'gainst Time's scythe can make defense
14 Save breed, to brave him when he takes thee hence.

---

1 *count . . . clock* keep track of the chimes; *tells* (1) counts, (2) recounts
2 *brave* splendid 4 *sable* black 6 *erst* formerly 7 *green* wheat (implying
youth) 9 *question make* speculate 10 *wastes of time* (1) things destroyed by
time, (2) wastelands of time, (3) results of wasted time 11 *themselves forsake*
(1) give themselves up to death, (2) abandon their true selves 14 *breed* off-
spring; *brave* defy

13

O, that you were your self, but, love, you are   1
No longer yours than you yourself here live:
Against this coming end you should prepare,   3
And your sweet semblance to some other give.
So should that beauty which you hold in lease   5
Find no determination; then you were   6
Your self again after yourself's decease
When your sweet issue your sweet form should bear.   8
Who lets so fair a house fall to decay,
Which husbandry in honor might uphold   10
Against the stormy gusts of winter's day
And barren rage of death's eternal cold?   12
   O, none but unthrifts, dear my love, you know,   13
   You had a father – let your son say so.

1, 7 *self* soul, immortal or essential self 3 *Against* in preparation for 5 *in lease* i.e., only for a limited period 6 *determination* end 8 *issue* children 10 *husbandry* economy (punning on "being a husband") 12 *barren rage* violence that results in barrenness 13 *unthrifts* spendthrifts

14

1 Not from the stars do I my judgment pluck,
2 And yet methinks I have astronomy –
3 But not to tell of good or evil luck,
    Of plagues, of dearths, or seasons' quality;
5 Nor can I fortune to brief minutes tell,
6 Pointing to each his thunder, rain, and wind,
    Or say with princes if it shall go well
8 By oft predict that I in heaven find;
    But from thine eyes my knowledge I derive,
10 And, constant stars, in them I read such art
11 As truth and beauty shall together thrive
12 If from thyself to store thou wouldst convert:
    Or else of thee this I prognosticate,
14   Thy end is truth's and beauty's doom and date.

---

1 *my . . . pluck* "get my opinions" (the tone is contemptuous) 2 *have astronomy* can do astrology 3 *not to tell* i.e., I don't use it as ordinary astrologers do 5 *fortune . . . tell* predict good and bad luck down to the minute 6 *Pointing* assigning; *his* its 8 *oft . . . that* frequent prediction of what 10 *read . . . art* find such knowledge 11 *As* as, for example, that 12 *store* provision, breeding; *convert* turn 14 *date* limit, end

15

When I consider everything that grows
Holds in perfection but a little moment,   2
That this huge stage presenteth nought but shows
Whereon the stars in secret influence comment;   4
When I perceive that men as plants increase,
Cheerèd and checked even by the selfsame sky,   6
Vaunt in their youthful sap, at height decrease,   7
And wear their brave state out of memory: 8
Then the conceit of this inconstant stay   9
Sets you most rich in youth before my sight,   10
Where wasteful Time debateth with Decay   11
To change your day of youth to sullied night;
  And, all in war with Time for love of you,
  As he takes from you, I engraft you new.   14

---

2 *Holds* stays   4 *Whereon . . . comment* i.e., which the stars inscrutably con-
trol (taking the astrology dismissed in Sonnet 14 seriously)   6 *Cheerèd and
checked* (1) applauded and hissed, (2) encouraged and held back   7 *Vaunt*
exult   8 *brave state* splendid finery; *out of memory* until it is forgotten   9
conceit thought; *inconstant stay* continual mutability   11 *with* together with
(Time and Decay are both debating *against* the poet)   14 *engraft you* infuse
new life into you (through my poems about you)

16

But wherefore do not you a mightier way
Make war upon this bloody tyrant Time?
3 And fortify yourself in your decay
With means more blessèd than my barren rhyme?
5 Now stand you on the top of happy hours,
6 And many maiden gardens, yet unset,
7 With virtuous wish would bear your living flowers,
8 Much liker than your painted counterfeit:
9 So should the lines of life that life repair
10 Which this (Time's pencil or my pupil pen)
11 Neither in inward worth nor outward fair
12 Can make you live yourself in eyes of men.
13   To give away yourself keeps yourself still,
        And you must live, drawn by your own sweet skill.

---

3 *in . . . decay* as you decay 5 *on the top* at the peak 6 *yet unset* not yet
seeded 7 *wish* willingness 8 *liker* more like you; *counterfeit* portrait 9
lines of life i.e., family lineage 10 *this (Time's . . . pen)* the sonnet (conceived
either as a portrait drawn by Time or the poet's verbal copy; most editors
delete the parentheses, rewriting the line and weakening the sense); *pencil*
small paintbrush (the pencil was normally a drawing instrument, the pen
normally a writing one) 11 *fair* beauty 12 *live yourself* i.e., actually live, as
opposed to living through the sonnet 13 *give . . . yourself* (1) give yourself
in marriage, (2) transfer yourself into your children

17

Who will believe my verse in time to come
If it were filled with your most high deserts? 2
Though yet, heaven knows, it is but as a tomb
Which hides your life and shows not half your parts. 4
If I could write the beauty of your eyes
And in fresh numbers number all your graces, 6
The age to come would say, "This poet lies –
Such heavenly touches ne'er touched earthly faces." 8
So should my papers, yellowed with their age,
Be scorned, like old men of less truth than tongue, 10
And your true rights be termed a poet's rage 11
And stretchèd meter of an antique song. 12
    But were some child of yours alive that time, 13
    You should live twice – in it and in my rhyme.

---

2 *deserts* (pronounced to rhyme with *parts*) 4 *parts* excellent qualities
6 *numbers* verses 8 *touches* artistic strokes 11 *your . . . rights* i.e., the praise
rightfully due to you 12 *stretchèd meter* poetic hyperbole; *antique song* old-
fashioned poem 13 *that time* in *time to come* (l. 1)

18

Shall I compare thee to a summer's day?
Thou art more lovely and more temperate.
Rough winds do shake the darling buds of May,
4   And summer's lease hath all too short a date.
Sometime too hot the eye of heaven shines,
And often is his gold complexion dimmed;
7   And every fair from fair sometime declines,
8   By chance, or nature's changing course, untrimmed:
But thy eternal summer shall not fade
10   Nor lose possession of that fair thou ow'st,
11   Nor shall Death brag thou wander'st in his shade
12   When in eternal lines to time thou grow'st.
        So long as men can breathe or eyes can see,
        So long lives this, and this gives life to thee.

---

4 *lease* allotted time; *date* duration   7 *fair* . . . *fair* beautiful thing from
beauty   8 *untrimmed* stripped of adornment   10 *fair* . . . *ow'st* beauty you
own   11 *shade* darkness   12 *to time* to the end of time

19

Devouring Time, blunt thou the lion's paws,   1
And make the earth devour her own sweet brood;   2
Pluck the keen teeth from the fierce tiger's jaws,
And burn the long-lived phoenix in her blood;   4
Make glad and sorry seasons as thou fleet'st,
And do whate'er thou wilt, swift-footed Time,
To the wide world and all her fading sweets,
But I forbid thee one most heinous crime:
O, carve not with thy hours my love's fair brow,
Nor draw no lines there with thine antique pen;   10
Him in thy course untainted do allow   11
For beauty's pattern to succeeding men.   12
    Yet do thy worst, old Time: despite thy wrong,
    My love shall in my verse ever live young.

---

1 *Devouring Time* (proverbially "Time consumes all things") 2 *brood* all
earthly things, conceived as children of "mother earth" 4 *phoenix* mythical
bird that lives for centuries, consumes itself in fire, and is reborn from its
ashes (hence symbolic of immortality); *in . . . blood* alive 10 *antique* (1) an-
cient, (2) antic, capricious, (3) causing one to be old, antiquing; *pen* writing,
not drawing, instrument (hence the *lines* are those of Time considered as a
hostile poet) 11 *untainted* (1) unsullied, (2) not struck by Time's lance (a
taint is a hit in jousting) 12 *pattern* ideal model

20

1 A woman's face, with Nature's own hand painted,
2 Hast thou, the master mistress of my passion;
A woman's gentle heart, but not acquainted
With shifting change, as is false women's fashion;
5 An eye more bright than theirs, less false in rolling,
6 Gilding the object whereupon it gazeth;
7 A man in hue all hues in his controlling,
Which steals men's eyes and women's souls amazeth.
9 And for a woman wert thou first created,
10 Till Nature as she wrought thee fell a-doting,
11 And by addition me of thee defeated
12 By adding one thing to my purpose nothing.
13 But since she pricked thee out for women's pleasure,
Mine be thy love, and thy love's use their treasure.

An alternative modernization of the final couplet:

13a But since she pricked thee out for women's pleasure,
14a Mine be thy love, and thy loves use their treasure.

---

1 *with . . . hand* i.e., naturally, without cosmetics   2 *master mistress* (1) both master and mistress, (2) prime mistress, (3) male lover   5 *rolling* roving, wandering   6 *Gilding* brightening   7 *hue* (1) form, (2) appearance, complexion; *in . . . controlling* (1) in his own power, (2) dominating (all other *hues*) by his appearance   9 *for* (1) as, (2) to be used by   11 *defeated* deprived, cheated   12 *to . . . nothing* useless for my purposes   13 *pricked . . . out* (1) selected you, "checked you off" (items to be marked on a sheet of paper were indicated by a pinprick), (2) furnished you with a penis   13a–14a (Lines 13–14 give the standard modernization since the late eighteenth century. But there is no reason to assume that Q's "loues" is a possessive rather than a plural, and that "vse" is a noun rather than a verb.)   13a *But . . . pleasure* however, since she selected you to experience pleasure as women do   14a *thy loves use* may your lovers use

20

A Womans face with natures owne hand painted,
  Haſte thou the Maſter Miſtris of my paſſion,
A womans gentle hart but not acquainted
With ſhifting change as is falſe womens faſhion,
An eye more bright then theirs, leſſe falſe in rowling:
Gilding the obiect where-vpon it gazeth,
A man in hew all *Hews* in his controwling,
Which ſteales mens eyes and womens ſoules amaſeth,
And for a woman wert thou firſt created,
Till nature as ſhe wrought thee fell a dotinge,
And by addition me of thee defeated,
By adding one thing to my purpoſe nothing.
   But ſince ſhe prickt thee out for womens pleaſure,
   Mine be thy loue and thy loues vſe their treaſure.

Sonnet 20 as it appears in the 1609 quarto.

21

1 So is it not with me as with that muse
2 Stirred by a painted beauty to his verse,
Who heaven itself for ornament doth use
4 And every fair with his fair doth rehearse;
5 Making a couplement of proud compare
With sun and moon, with earth and sea's rich gems,
7 With April's first-born flowers, and all things rare
8 That heaven's air in this huge rondure hems.
O let me, true in love, but truly write,
10 And then believe me, my love is as fair
As any mother's child, though not so bright
12 As those gold candles fixed in heaven's air:
13   Let them say more that like of hearsay well;
14   I will not praise that purpose not to sell.

---

1 *muse* poet (here masculine) 2 *Stirred* inspired; *painted beauty* beauty achieved through artifice (whether in a portrait or through the use of cosmetics) 4 *every . . . rehearse* names every other beautiful thing along with the beautiful subject of his poem; *rehearse* enumerate, mention 5 *proud* (1) splendid, (2) presumptuous; *compare* comparison 7 *rare* precious 8 *rondure* sphere; *hems* encircles 12 *gold candles* i.e., stars 13 *hearsay* second-hand or unfounded reports 14 *that . . . not* since I do not intend (i.e., I am not advertising you for sale)

22

My glass shall not persuade me I am old
So long as youth and thou are of one date;   2
But when in thee time's furrows I behold,
Then look I death my days should expiate.   4
For all that beauty that doth cover thee
Is but the seemly raiment of my heart,   6
Which in thy breast doth live, as thine in me:
How can I then be elder than thou art?
O therefore, love, be of thyself so wary
As I, not for myself, but for thee will,   10
Bearing thy heart, which I will keep so chary   11
As tender nurse her babe from faring ill.
    Presume not on thy heart when mine is slain;   13
    Thou gav'st me thine not to give back again.

---

2 *of one date* the same age ("as young as youth itself")   4 *expiate* conclude, bring peace to   6 *seemly raiment* beautiful and appropriate covering   10 *will* will be   11 *chary* carefully   13 *Presume . . . on* do not expect to recover

23

1 As an unperfect actor on the stage,
2 Who with his fear is put besides his part,
3 Or some fierce thing replete with too much rage,
4 Whose strength's abundance weakens his own heart;
5 So I, for fear of trust, forget to say
6 The perfect ceremony of love's rite,
7 And in mine own love's strength seem to decay,
O'ercharged with burden of mine own love's might.
9 O, let my books be then the eloquence
10 And dumb presagers of my speaking breast,
Who plead for love, and look for recompense,
12 More than that tongue that more hath more expressed.
O, learn to read what silent love hath writ:
14 To hear with eyes belongs to love's fine wit.

---

1 *an unperfect actor* (1) one who has not adequately learned his lines, (2) one who has not mastered the craft of acting 2 *fear* stage fright; *put besides* put off, made to forget 3 *replete . . . rage* overwhelmed with violent anger 4 *Whose* (the antecedent is *rage*, not *thing*); *heart* (1) courage, (2) ability to act 5 *for . . . trust* (1) distrusting myself, (2) doubting that I will be believed, (3) overcome with the responsibility 6 *perfect ceremony* word-perfect ritual; *love's rite* the ceremony due to love (*love's rite* normally means sexual intercourse, and that is certainly at least an overtone here – Q has "right"; the two words were not distinguished in Shakespeare's time) 7 *mine . . . strength* (1) the force of my passion, (2) the power of my beloved; *decay* falter, weaken 9 *books* writings 10 *dumb presagers* (1) silent messages, (2) mute heralds 12 *more hath more expressed* more often has said more 14 *wit* (1) intelligence, (2) poetic skill

24

Mine eye hath played the painter and hath steeled   1
Thy beauty's form in table of my heart;   2
My body is the frame wherein 'tis held,
And perspective it is best painter's art.   4
For through the painter must you see his skill
To find where your true image pictured lies,
Which in my bosom's shop is hanging still,   7
That hath his windows glazèd with thine eyes.   8
Now see what good turns eyes for eyes have done:
Mine eyes have drawn thy shape, and thine for me   10
Are windows to my breast, wherethrough the sun
Delights to peep, to gaze therein on thee.
    Yet eyes this cunning want to grace their art;   13
    They draw but what they see, know not the heart.

---

1 *steeled* engraved, permanently drawn (emended by most editors to "stelled," portrayed) 2 *table* tablet (any writing or drawing surface) 4 *perspective* realistic depiction 7 *still* (1) always, (2) continuously, (3) as before 8 *his* its 13 *this . . . want* lack this skill

reading this one

25

1 Let those who are in favor with their stars
Of public honor and proud titles boast,
Whilst I, whom fortune of such triumph bars,
4 Unlooked for joy in that I honor most.
Great princes' favorites their fair leaves spread
6 But as the marigold at the sun's eye;
7 And in themselves their pride lies burièd,
For at a frown they in their glory die.
9 The painful warrior famousèd for fight,
10 After a thousand victories once foiled,
11 Is from the book of honor razèd quite,
And all the rest forgot for which he toiled.
Then happy I, that love and am beloved
14 Where I may not remove nor be removed.

---

1 *who . . . stars* whose stars are propitious 4 *Unlooked for* (1) unexpectedly,
(2) unnoticed; *joy . . . most* (1) delight in what I honor most, (2) take plea-
sure in the fact that I am most devoted 6 *But* merely 7 *in themselves* on
their own, left to themselves; *pride* (1) splendor, (2) self-esteem 9 *painful*
(1) painstaking, (2) in pain; *fight* (the usual emendation for Q's "worth";
some editors retain "worth" and emend the rhyme word *quite* in l. 11 to
"forth") 10 *once foiled* defeated only once 11 *razèd* expunged, erased 14
remove leave; *removed* dismissed

26

Lord of my love, to whom in vassalage
Thy merit hath my duty strongly knit,
To thee I send this written ambassage   3
To witness duty, not to show my wit;   4
Duty so great, which wit so poor as mine   5
May make seem bare, in wanting words to show it,   6
But that I hope some good conceit of thine   7
In thy soul's thought, all naked, will bestow it;   8
Till whatsoever star that guides my moving   9
Points on me graciously with fair aspect,   10
And puts apparel on my tattered loving
To show me worthy of thy sweet respect:
    Then may I dare to boast how I do love thee;
    Till then not show my head where thou mayst prove me.   14

1–2 *Lord . . . knit* (the poem uses the language of formal dedications)   3 *ambassage* message carried by an ambassador (normally oral)   4 *wit* (1) cleverness, (2) poetic skill   5 *wit* intelligence   6 *bare* meager, insufficient; *wanting* lacking   7 *But* except; *good conceit* (1) kind opinion, (2) ingenious poetic thought   8 *all . . . it* will house (or employ) it despite its nakedness   9 *moving* actions   10 *Points* shines; *fair aspect* favorable astrological influence   14 *prove* test

27

Weary with toil, I haste me to my bed,
2 The dear repose for limbs with travel tired,
   But then begins a journey in my head
4 To work my mind when body's work's expired;
5 For then my thoughts, from far where I abide,
6 Intend a zealous pilgrimage to thee,
   And keep my drooping eyelids open wide,
8 Looking on darkness which the blind do see;
9 Save that my soul's imaginary sight
10 Presents thy shadow to my sightless view,
11 Which, like a jewel hung in ghastly night,
   Makes black night beauteous and her old face new.
    Lo, thus, by day my limbs, by night my mind,
    For thee and for myself no quiet find.

2 *travel* (1) journeying, (2) travail, labor   4 *work* (1) put to work, (2) distress
5 *from far* from the distant place   6 *Intend* (1) set out on, (2) determine on
8 *which* such as   9 *imaginary* (1) imaginative, (2) unreal   10 *shadow* image
11 *ghastly* ghostly, terrifying

28

How can I then return in happy plight   1
That am debarred the benefit of rest,
When day's oppression is not eased by night,
But day by night and night by day oppressed,
And each, though enemies to either's reign,   5
Do in consent shake hands to torture me,   6
The one by toil, the other to complain   7
How far I toil, still farther off from thee?
I tell the day to please him thou art bright   9
And dost him grace when clouds do blot the heaven;   10
So flatter I the swart complexioned night,   11
When sparkling stars twire not, thou gild'st the even.   12
   But day doth daily draw my sorrows longer,
   And night doth nightly make grief's length seem   14
   stronger.

---

1 *happy plight* good shape 5 *either's* each other's 6 *shake hands* unite, agree
7 *to complain* by causing me to complain 9 *I . . . bright* (1) I tell the day
that the reason you are bright is to please him, (2) I tell the day, in order to
please him, that you are bright 10 *dost . . . grace* are gracious to him – i.e.,
shine on him (*grace* is a noun, not a verb) 11 *swart* dark 12 *twire* peep;
even evening 14 *length* (unnecessarily emended by most editors to
"strength")

29

1 When, in disgrace with fortune and men's eyes,
   I all alone beweep my outcast state,
3 And trouble deaf heaven with my bootless cries,
   And look upon myself and curse my fate,
   Wishing me like to one more rich in hope,
6 Featured like him, like him with friends possessed,
7 Desiring this man's art, and that man's scope,
8 With what I most enjoy contented least;
   Yet in these thoughts myself almost despising,
10 Haply I think on thee, and then my state,
   Like to the lark at break of day arising
12 From sullen earth, sings hymns at heaven's gate;
     For thy sweet love remembered such wealth brings
     That then I scorn to change my state with kings.

---

1 *in disgrace* out of favor 3 *bootless* useless 6 *like him, like him* like one man, like another 7 *art* (1) skill, (2) learning, (3) practical ability; *scope* (1) independence, (2) range of ability, (3) breadth of opportunity 8 *enjoy* (1) possess, (2) take pleasure in 10 *Haply* by chance 12 *sullen* (1) dull, heavy, (2) somber, sad

30

When to the sessions of sweet silent thought   1
I summon up remembrance of things past,
I sigh the lack of many a thing I sought,   3
And with old woes new wail my dear time's waste: 4
Then can I drown an eye, unused to flow,
For precious friends hid in death's dateless night,   6
And weep afresh love's long since canceled woe,   7
And moan th' expense of many a vanished sight.   8
Then can I grieve at grievances foregone,   9
And heavily from woe to woe tell o'er   10
The sad account of forebemoanèd moan,   11
Which I new pay as if not paid before.
    But if the while I think on thee, dear friend,
    All losses are restored and sorrows end.

---

1 *sessions* periodic sittings of a court (cf. *summon*, l. 2; his *thought* is the judge) 3 *sigh* lament 4 *new* newly; *dear . . . waste* (1) precious time's passing, (2) destruction of precious things by time, (3) the fact that my best time is destroyed (taking Q's "times" as a plural rather than a possessive) 6 *dateless* endless 7 *canceled* fully paid off 8 *expense* (1) expenditure, (2) loss 9 *foregone* in the past, over and done with 10 *heavily* (1) sorrowfully, (2) tediously; *tell o'er* (1) add up, (2) recount 11 *account* (1) bill, (2) narrative; *forebemoanèd moan* already lamented grief

31

1 Thy bosom is endearèd with all hearts
2 Which I by lacking have supposèd dead;
3 And there reigns love, and all love's loving parts,
   And all those friends which I thought burièd.
5 How many a holy and obsequious tear
6 Hath dear religious love stol'n from mine eye,
7 As interest of the dead, which now appear
8 But things removed that hidden in thee lie!
   Thou art the grave where buried love doth live,
10 Hung with the trophies of my lovers gone,
11 Who all their parts of me to thee did give;
12 That due of many now is thine alone.
    Their images I loved I view in thee,
14 And thou, all they, hast all the all of me.

---

1 *endearèd* enriched   2 *by lacking* (i.e., who have died)   3 *love's . . . parts* all
the attributes of his other loves (with the innuendo of *loving parts* as sexual
organs)   5 *obsequious* dutifully mourning   6 *dear* deeply felt; *religious* (1)
pious, (2) assiduous   7 *interest of* what is due to; *which* who   8 *removed* who
have moved   10 *trophies* memorials; *lovers* (the word had a broad range of
meaning, from "dear friends [of either sex]" to "seekers or recipients of pa-
tronage" to "sexual partners," and everything in between)   11 *parts of* shares
in (with the same overtone as in l. 3)   12 *That . . . many* what was owed to
many   14 *all they* who include them all

32

If thou survive my well-contented day   1
When that churl Death my bones with dust shall cover,
And shalt by fortune once more resurvey   3
These poor rude lines of thy deceasèd lover,   4
Compare them with the bett'ring of the time,   5
And though they be outstripped by every pen,
Reserve them for my love, not for their rhyme,   7
Exceeded by the height of happier men.   8
O, then vouchsafe me but this loving thought:
Had my friend's muse grown with this growing age,   10
A dearer birth than this his love had brought   11
To march in ranks of better equipage;   12
   But since he died, and poets better prove,
   Theirs for their style I'll read, his for his love.

---

1 *well-contented* (1) final, (2) willingly arrived at (the metaphor is financial: a *contented* debt is one fully paid off) 3 *fortune* chance 4 *lover* (see note on 31.10) 5 *bett'ring* progress, refinement 7 *Reserve* preserve; *rhyme* poetry 8 *height* achievement; *happier* (1) luckier, (2) more accomplished 11 *dearer birth* i.e., more precious poem; *brought* brought forth 12 *ranks . . . equipage* i.e., in company with more elegant verse

33

Full many a glorious morning have I seen
2 Flatter the mountain tops with sovereign eye,
Kissing with golden face the meadows green,
Gilding pale streams with heavenly alchemy;
5 Anon permit the basest clouds to ride
6 With ugly rack on his celestial face,
And from the forlorn world his visage hide,
8 Stealing unseen to west with this disgrace:
Even so my sun one early morn did shine
10 With all-triumphant splendor on my brow;
11 But, out alack, he was but one hour mine,
12 The region cloud hath masked him from me now.
13   Yet him for this my love no whit disdaineth;
14   Suns of the world may stain when heaven's sun staineth.

---

2 *Flatter* (1) caress, (2) praise dishonestly 5 *Anon* soon 6 *rack* streaks of cloud 8 *disgrace* (1) dishonor, (2) withdrawal of favor 11 *out alack* alas 12 *region cloud* clouds where he now is 13 *no whit* not at all 14 *stain* (1) offend, (2) be stained

34

Why didst thou promise such a beauteous day
And make me travel forth without my cloak,
To let base clouds o'ertake me in my way,   3
Hiding thy brav'ry in their rotten smoke?   4
'Tis not enough that through the cloud thou break
To dry the rain on my storm-beaten face,
For no man well of such a salve can speak
That heals the wound, and cures not the disgrace: 8
Nor can thy shame give physic to my grief;   9
Though thou repent, yet I have still the loss: 10
Th' offender's sorrow lends but weak relief
To him that bears the strong offense's cross.
    Ah, but those tears are pearl which thy love sheeds,   13
    And they are rich and ransom all ill deeds.   14

---

3 *base* (1) dark, (2) dishonorable   4 *brav'ry* splendor; *rotten smoke* unwholesome mists   8 *disgrace* (1) shame, (2) disfigurement (the scar left by the *wound*)   9 *shame* regret; *physic* remedy   13 *sheeds* sheds   14 *ransom* (1) atone for, (2) redeem

35

No more be grieved at that which thou hast done:
Roses have thorns, and silver fountains mud;
3 Clouds and eclipses stain both moon and sun,
4 And loathsome canker lives in sweetest bud.
5 All men make faults, and even I in this,
6 Authorizing thy trespass with compare,
7 Myself corrupting, salving thy amiss,
8 Excusing thy sins more than thy sins are;
9 For to thy sensual fault I bring in sense –
10 Thy adverse party is thy advocate –
11 And 'gainst myself a lawful plea commence;
Such civil war is in my love and hate
That I an accessary needs must be
14 To that sweet thief which sourly robs from me.

---

3 *stain* darken 4 *canker* cankerworm (caterpillar, or its larva, that destroys the rosebud from within) 5 *make faults* (1) make mistakes, (2) commit sins 6 *Authorizing* justifying; *with compare* through comparisons 7 *salving* palliating, explaining away; *amiss* offense 8 *Excusing . . . are* going further in excusing your sins than you go in sinning 9 *sensual* physical (not intellectual, hence with overtones of sexuality and lust); *sense* (1) reason, (2) feeling (and hence, *hurt* feelings) 10 *adverse party* adversary (i.e., myself) 11 *lawful* (1) legal, (2) just 14 *sourly* (punning on "sorely," a homonym in Elizabethan English)

36

Let me confess that we two must be twain
Although our undivided loves are one:
So shall those blots that do with me remain,   3
Without thy help by me be borne alone.   4
In our two loves there is but one respect,   5
Though in our lives a separable spite,   6
Which though it alter not love's sole effect,   7
Yet doth it steal sweet hours from love's delight.
I may not evermore acknowledge thee,
Lest my bewailèd guilt should do thee shame;   10
Nor thou with public kindness honor me
Unless thou take that honor from thy name: 12
   But do not so; I love thee in such sort   13
   As, thou being mine, mine is thy good report. 14

---

3 *blots* disgraces, shames (cf. Sonnets 29, 33–35) 4 *by . . . alone* (1) be en-
dured only by me, (2) be endured by me in solitude 5 *respect* (1) concern,
(2) reputation, (3) consideration, (4) esteem 6 *separable spite* (1) vexation
that separates us, (2) separation that spites us 7 *sole effect* singleness (cf. *one
respect*, l. 5), unique character 10 *bewailèd* lamented 12 *Unless . . . name*
i.e., without dishonoring yourself 13–14 *But . . . report* (the same couplet
concludes Sonnet 96) 13 *in . . . sort* in such a way 14 *report* reputation

37

As a decrepit father takes delight
To see his active child do deeds of youth,
3   So I, made lame by fortune's dearest spite,
4   Take all my comfort of thy worth and truth.
5   For whether beauty, birth, or wealth, or wit,
Or any of these all, or all, or more,
7   Entitled in thy parts do crownèd sit,
8   I make my love engrafted to this store.
So then I am not lame, poor, nor despised
10 Whilst that this shadow doth such substance give
11 That I in thy abundance am sufficed
And by a part of all thy glory live.
13   Look what is best, that best I wish in thee.
This wish I have; then ten times happy me!

---

3 *made lame* disabled; *dearest spite* worst, most costly malice   4 *of* from;
truth (1) fidelity, (2) honesty, (3) honorableness   5 *wit* intelligence   7 *Enti-
tled . . . sit* are enthroned among your virtues   8 *I . . . store* I graft my love
onto this abundance (and thus both contribute to it and am nourished by it)
10 *shadow* idea, image; *substance* reality (reversing the normal order, in which
the *substance* produces the *shadow*)   11 *sufficed* satisfied   13 *Look what*
whatever

38

How can my muse want subject to invent   1
While thou dost breathe, that pour'st into my verse
Thine own sweet argument, too excellent   3
For every vulgar paper to rehearse?   4
O, give thyself the thanks if aught in me   5
Worthy perusal stand against thy sight,   6
For who's so dumb that cannot write to thee
When thou thyself dost give invention light?   8
Be thou the tenth muse, ten times more in worth   9
Than those old nine which rhymers invocate;   10
And he that calls on thee, let him bring forth
Eternal numbers to outlive long date.   12
   If my slight muse do please these curious days,   13
    The pain be mine, but thine shall be the praise. 14

---

1 *want . . . invent* be unable to find a subject (in rhetoric, *inventio* was the essential first step in the process of composition, the finding of a topic) 3 *Thine . . . argument* the sweet theme of yourself 4 *vulgar paper* commonplace composition; *rehearse* declare, repeat 5 *aught . . . me* anything of mine 6 *stand against* (1) meet, (2) withstand, stand up to 8 *invention* poetic creation 9 *tenth muse* (in addition to the traditional nine muses, daughters of Zeus and Mnemosyne, and patronesses of learning and the arts) 10 *which . . . invocate* (poets traditionally began by invoking the muse) 12 *numbers* verses; *outlive . . . date* live beyond even a distant date 13 *curious* supercritical, aesthetically demanding 14 *pain* effort

39

1 O, how thy worth with manners may I sing
2 When thou art all the better part of me?
What can mine own praise to mine own self bring,
And what is't but mine own when I praise thee?
5 Even for this let us divided live
6 And our dear love lose name of single one,
That by this separation I may give
8 That due to thee which thou deserv'st alone.
9 O absence, what a torment wouldst thou prove
10 Were it not thy sour leisure gave sweet leave
11 To entertain the time with thoughts of love,
12 Which time and thoughts so sweetly doth deceive,
13 And that thou teachest how to make one twain
14 By praising him here who doth hence remain.

---

1 *with manners* decently (i.e., as l. 2 explains, without praising myself)
2 *thou . . . me* ("A friend is a second self" was proverbial) 5 *Even for* precisely because of 6 *dear* (1) precious, (2) heartfelt; *lose . . . one* cease to be known as single or inseparable 8 *That* what is 9 *absence* (the proposed *divided* self of l. 5) 11 *entertain* pleasantly fill 12 *deceive* beguile 13 *that . . . twain* were it not that you teach us how to divide one into two 14 *here* (1) in the sonnet, (2) in this place (where I am)

40

Take all my loves, my love, yea, take them all: 1
What hast thou then more than thou hadst before?
No love, my love, that thou mayst true love call;   3
All mine was thine before thou hadst this more.
Then, if for my love thou my love receivest,   5
I cannot blame thee for my love thou usest;   6
But yet be blamed if thou this self deceivest   7
By willful taste of what thyself refusest.   8
I do forgive thy robb'ry, gentle thief,
Although thou steal thee all my poverty;   10
And yet love knows it is a greater grief
To bear love's wrong than hate's known injury.   12
    Lascivious grace, in whom all ill well shows,   13
    Kill me with spites; yet we must not be foes.   14

Sonnets 40–42 allude to a romantic betrayal of the sort much more intensely realized later in Sonnets 127–152, the so-called Dark Lady sonnets, especially 133, 134, and 144.
1 *Take . . . loves* (1) take all the love I have, (2) take all my other lovers for yourself 3 *No . . . call* i.e., no love other than mine is true; no lover is true except me 5 *for my love* (1) because it is what I love, (2) instead of my love; *my love receivest* accept my lover 6 *for . . . usest* (1) for the fact that you enjoy my love, (2) for the fact that you sleep with my mistress (the rival love is clearly a woman in Sonnets 41 and 42) 7 *this self* i.e., me, as opposed to your other self, you 8 *By . . . refusest* i.e., by willfully experiencing what you yourself refuse to others (or what you deep in your heart reject); *willful* (1) stubborn, (2) intentional, (3) lustful 10 *steal . . . poverty* take for yourself the little I have 12 *love's wrong* (1) a wrong done to love, (2) the wrong done by a lover; *known* intentional, overt 13 *Lascivious grace* (you who are) gracious even in lechery; *grace* charm, beauty 14 *spites* injuries, malice

41

1 Those pretty wrongs that liberty commits
  When I am sometime absent from thy heart,
3 Thy beauty and thy years full well befits,
4 For still temptation follows where thou art.
5 Gentle thou art, and therefore to be won;
  Beauteous thou art, therefore to be assailed;
  And when a woman woos, what woman's son
8 Will sourly leave her till he have prevailed?
9 Ay me, but yet thou mightst my seat forbear,
10 And chide thy beauty and thy straying youth,
11 Who lead thee in their riot even there
12 Where thou art forced to break a twofold truth:
    Hers, by thy beauty tempting her to thee,
    Thine, by thy beauty being false to me.

---

1 *pretty wrongs* charming peccadilloes; *liberty* license (the freedom of a libertine) 3 *befits* befit (the subject is *wrongs*) 4 *still* always 5 *Gentle* (1) gracious, (2) noble; *to be won* (1) able to be won, (2) worth winning 8 *he* (emended by most editors to "she," but the wit of the line lies in the recognition of who is really the winner) 9 *my . . . forbear* leave my place in your heart unoccupied 11 *riot* revelry, debauchery 12 *truth* troth, faith

THE SONNETS ❧ 45

42

That thou hast her, it is not all my grief,
And yet it may be said I loved her dearly;
That she hath thee is of my wailing chief,   3
A loss in love that touches me more nearly.   4
Loving offenders, thus I will excuse ye: 5
Thou dost love her because thou know'st I love her,
And for my sake even so doth she abuse me,   7
Suff'ring my friend for my sake to approve her.   8
If I lose thee, my loss is my love's gain,   9
And losing her, my friend hath found that loss: 10
Both find each other, and I lose both twain,
And both for my sake lay on me this cross.   12
    But here's the joy: my friend and I are one;
    Sweet flattery! then she loves but me alone.

---

3 *of . . . chief* my chief cause of complaint   4 *nearly* intimately   5 *excuse* (1)
make excuses for, (2) justify, (3) pardon   7 *abuse* betray (literally, "use me
badly")   8 *Suff'ring* allowing; *approve her* test her, try her out sexually   9 *my
love's* i.e., the mistress's   12 *cross* affliction

43

1 When most I wink, then do mine eyes best see,
2 For all the day they view things unrespected;
But when I sleep, in dreams they look on thee
4 And, darkly bright, are bright in dark directed.
5 Then thou, whose shadow shadows doth make bright,
6 How would thy shadow's form form happy show
7 To the clear day with thy much clearer light
When to unseeing eyes thy shade shines so!
How would, I say, mine eyes be blessèd made
10 By looking on thee in the living day,
11 When in dead night thy fair imperfect shade
Through heavy sleep on sightless eyes doth stay!
        All days are nights to see till I see thee,
14   And nights bright days when dreams do show thee me.

1 *wink* shut my eyes 2 *unrespected* ignored 4 *darkly* (1) secretly, (2) myste-
riously, (3) blindly; *bright* radiant (in Renaissance physiology, the eyes saw by
emitting light); *are bright in dark directed* i.e., see clearly in the darkness
5 *shadow* image; *shadows* darkness 6 *shadow's form* body (the substance of
which the shadow is an image); *form . . . show* create a pleasing sight 7 *clear*
bright 11 *imperfect* incomplete (because lacking a body) 14 *show . . . me*
show you to me

44

If the dull substance of my flesh were thought,   1
Injurious distance should not stop my way;   2
For then, despite of space, I would be brought,   3
From limits far remote, where thou dost stay.   4
No matter then although my foot did stand
Upon the farthest earth removed from thee;   6
For nimble thought can jump both sea and land
As soon as think the place where he would be.   8
But, ah, thought kills me that I am not thought,
To leap large lengths of miles when thou art gone,   10
But that, so much of earth and water wrought,   11
I must attend time's leisure with my moan,   12
    Receiving nought by elements so slow
    But heavy tears, badges of either's woe.   14

---

1 *dull* (1) sluggish, (2) heavy 2 *Injurious* spiteful; *stop* block 3 *despite* in spite 4 *limits* regions; *where* to where 6 *farthest . . . removed* point on earth farthest removed 8 *he* i.e., *thought* 11 *so much* being only so much; *earth . . . wrought* (in Renaissance humoral physiology, the bodily parts of the human organism were composed of the heavy elements earth and water, the intellect of the light elements air and fire) 12 *attend . . . leisure* (1) wait for time to pass, (2) wait till the time is right 14 *either's* i.e., of the heavy element *earth* and the wet element *water*

45

1 The other two, slight air and purging fire,
Are both with thee, wherever I abide;
The first my thought, the other my desire,
4 These present-absent with swift motion slide.
5 For when these quicker elements are gone
In tender embassy of love to thee,
My life, being made of four, with two alone
8 Sinks down to death, oppressed with melancholy;
9 Until life's composition be recured
10 By those swift messengers returned from thee,
Who even but now come back again, assured
Of thy fair health, recounting it to me.
    This told, I joy; but then no longer glad,
    I send them back again and straight grow sad.

---

1 *other two* i.e., other two elements (continuing the argument of Sonnet 44); *slight* insubstantial; *purging* purifying 4 *present-absent* always and alternately here and elsewhere 5 *quicker* (1) faster, (2) more alive 8 *melancholy* (the bodily humor associated with earth) 9 *life's . . . recured* the proper balance of humors is restored 10 *swift messengers* i.e., *air* and *fire*

46

Mine eye and heart are at a mortal war
How to divide the conquest of thy sight;   2
Mine eye my heart thy picture's sight would bar,   3
My heart mine eye the freedom of that right.   4
My heart doth plead that thou in him dost lie,
A closet never pierced with crystal eyes;   6
But the defendant doth that plea deny
And says in him thy fair appearance lies.
To 'cide this title is impanelèd   9
A quest of thoughts, all tenants to the heart,   10
And by their verdict is determinèd
The clear eye's moiety and the dear heart's part,   12
    As thus: mine eye's due is thy outward part,
    And my heart's right thy inward love of heart.

---

2 *conquest . . . sight* i.e., spoils of war, consisting of the sight of you (but *conquest* also means a legal acquisition by any means other than inheritance, a sense that becomes operative from l. 7 on) 3 *bar* prohibit 4 *freedom* free exercise 6 *closet* (1) small private room, study, (2) cabinet, strongbox 9 *'cide* decide; *title* legal right to possession (of what is acquired by the *conquest* of l. 2) 10 *quest* jury; *all . . . heart* the heart's dependents (hence, the jury is packed) 12 *moiety* share

47

1 Betwixt mine eye and heart a league is took,
And each doth good turns now unto the other:
When that mine eye is famished for a look,
4 Or heart in love with sighs himself doth smother,
With my love's picture then my eye doth feast
And to the painted banquet bids my heart;
Another time mine eye is my heart's guest
And in his thoughts of love doth share a part.
So, either by thy picture or my love,
10 Thyself away are present still with me;
For thou not farther than my thoughts canst move,
And I am still with them, and they with thee;
    Or, if they sleep, thy picture in my sight
    Awakes my heart to heart's and eye's delight.

---

1 *a . . . took* an alliance is made   4 *Or heart* or when my heart   10 *still* (1) always, (2) nevertheless

48

How careful was I, when I took my way,   1
Each trifle under truest bars to thrust,   2
That to my use it might unusèd stay   3
From hands of falsehood, in sure wards of trust!   4
But thou, to whom my jewels trifles are,   5
Most worthy comfort, now my greatest grief,
Thou best of dearest, and mine only care,   7
Art left the prey of every vulgar thief.   8
Thee have I not locked up in any chest,
Save where thou art not, though I feel thou art,   10
Within the gentle closure of my breast,   11
From whence at pleasure thou mayst come and part;
    And even thence thou wilt be stol'n, I fear,
    For truth proves thievish for a prize so dear.   14

---

1 *took my way* set out on my journey 2 *truest* strongest 3 *to* for 4 *hands of falsehood* i.e., thieves; *in . . . trust* (1) kept by trustworthy guards, (2) securely locked up 5 *to* in comparison with 7 *mine . . . care* the only thing I value 8 *vulgar* common 11 *closure* enclosure 14 *truth* honesty itself; *dear* precious

49

1 Against that time, if ever that time come,
   When I shall see thee frown on my defects,
3 Whenas thy love hath cast his utmost sum,
4 Called to that audit by advised respects;
5 Against that time when thou shalt strangely pass
   And scarcely greet me with that sun, thine eye,
   When love, converted from the thing it was,
8 Shall reasons find of settled gravity:
9 Against that time do I ensconce me here
10 Within the knowledge of mine own desert,
11 And this my hand against myself uprear
12 To guard the lawful reasons on thy part.
   To leave poor me thou hast the strength of laws,
14 Since why to love I can allege no cause.

---

1 *Against* in preparation for 3 *Whenas* when; *hath . . . sum* has made its
final reckoning, closed its account 4 *advised respects* carefully considered
reasoning 5 *strangely* like a stranger, unfriendly 8 *of . . . gravity* (1) of suf-
ficient seriousness, (2) for continued reserve (toward me) 9 *ensconce* fortify
10 *desert* merit (rhymes with *part*) 11 *this . . . uprear* (1) as a witness, swear
against myself, (2) as a soldier, threaten myself 12 *the . . . part* the justice of
your arguments 14 *why to love* why you should love me; *no cause* no reason
(but cf. Cordelia's "No cause, no cause," *King Lear,* IV.7.78: real love needs
no reasons)

50

How heavy do I journey on the way 1
When what I seek (my weary travel's end) 2
Doth teach that ease and that repose to say 3
Thus far the miles are measured from thy friend.
The beast that bears me, tired with my woe,
Plods dully on, to bear that weight in me, 6
As if by some instinct the wretch did know
His rider loved not speed, being made from thee. 8
The bloody spur cannot provoke him on
That sometimes anger thrusts into his hide, 10
Which heavily he answers with a groan,
More sharp to me than spurring to his side; 12
    For that same groan doth put this in my mind:
    My grief lies onward and my joy behind.

---

1 *heavy* (1) sadly, (2) wearily 2 *travel's* (1) journey's, (2) toil's 3 *that ease . . . repose* i.e., the rest at the journey's end 6 *dully* (the standard modernization of Q's "duly," dutifully, because of *my dull bearer,* 51.2; but since both were possible spellings of both words, both meanings would have been implied for the seventeenth-century reader) 8 *made* carried away 12 *sharp* painful

51

1 Thus can my love excuse the slow offense
2 Of my dull bearer when from thee I speed:
  From where thou art why should I haste me thence?
4 Till I return, of posting is no need.
5 O, what excuse will my poor beast then find
6 When swift extremity can seem but slow?
  Then should I spur, though mounted on the wind,
8 In wingèd speed no motion shall I know.
  Then can no horse with my desire keep pace;
10 Therefore desire, of perfect'st love being made,
11 Shall neigh no dull flesh in his fiery race;
12 But love, for love, thus shall excuse my jade:
13   Since from thee going he went willful slow,
14   Towards thee I'll run and give him leave to go.

1 *love* affection, passion (not the lover); *slow offense* offensive slowness   2 *speed* i.e., even slowness is too fast   4 *posting* riding fast   5 *then* (on my return journey)   6 *swift extremity* extreme speed   8 *In . . . know* flying like the wind, I'll still feel I'm not moving   11 *neigh . . . flesh* i.e., express nothing bodily (Q's "naigh" is often emended to "weigh," which does nothing to clarify a puzzling line)   12 *for love* (1) for its own sake, (2) in repayment of love, (3) in anticipation of love, etc.; *jade* weary horse   13 *willful* willfully   14 *go* walk (i.e., I'll race back without him)

52

So am I as the rich whose blessèd key   1
Can bring him to his sweet up-lockèd treasure,
The which he will not every hour survey,
For blunting the fine point of seldom pleasure.   4
Therefore are feasts so solemn and so rare,   5
Since, seldom coming, in the long year set,
Like stones of worth they thinly placèd are,   7
Or captain jewels in the carcanet.   8
So is the time that keeps you as my chest,   9
Or as the wardrobe which the robe doth hide,   10
To make some special instant special blessed
By new unfolding his imprisoned pride.   12
　　Blessèd are you, whose worthiness gives scope,
　　Being had, to triumph, being lacked, to hope.

---

1 *rich* rich man   4 *For* for fear of; *seldom pleasure* pleasure seldom enjoyed
5 *solemn* (1) ceremonious, (2) significant   7 *thinly* sparsely   8 *captain* main,
most important; *carcanet* necklace or jeweled collar   9 *as . . . chest* like my
treasure chest   12 *new* newly; *his* its (the *time's*, l. 9)

53

1 What is your substance, whereof are you made,
2 That millions of strange shadows on you tend?
Since every one hath, every one, one shade,
4 And you, but one, can every shadow lend.
5 Describe Adonis, and the counterfeit
Is poorly imitated after you.
7 On Helen's cheek all art of beauty set,
8 And you in Grecian tires are painted new.
9 Speak of the spring and foison of the year:
10 The one doth shadow of your beauty show,
The other as your bounty doth appear,
12 And you in every blessèd shape we know.
    In all external grace you have some part,
    But you like none, none you, for constant heart.

---

1 *substance* physical nature (as opposed, in Platonic philosophy, to *shadow,* appearance) 2 *strange* foreign – i.e., not belonging to your substance; *tend* attend 4 *you . . . lend* i.e., every shadow can reflect only a single version of you 5 *Adonis* the ideally beautiful youth wooed by Venus (see Ovid, *Metamorphoses* X.298–559, 708–39, and Shakespeare's poem *Venus and Adonis*) 5–6 *counterfeit . . . after* portrait is a poor imitation of 7 *On . . . set* employ all the beauty of art to depict Helen's face 8 *tires* garments; *new* newly 9 *foison* harvest 12 *blessèd* gracious, handsome; *know* recognize

54

O, how much more doth beauty beauteous seem
By that sweet ornament which truth doth give: 2
The rose looks fair, but fairer we it deem
For that sweet odor which doth in it live.
The canker blooms have full as deep a dye 5
As the perfumèd tincture of the roses, 6
Hang on such thorns, and play as wantonly 7
When summer's breath their maskèd buds discloses; 8
But, for their virtue only is their show, 9
They live unwooed and unrespected fade, 10
Die to themselves. Sweet roses do not so: 11
Of their sweet deaths are sweetest odors made.
    And so of you, beauteous and lovely youth,
    When that shall vade, by verse distills your truth. 14

---

2 *By* by means of 5 *canker blooms* canker roses or dog roses (*Rosa canina*), prickly wild roses with little scent 6 *tincture* color 7 *wantonly* (1) playfully, (2) lasciviously 8 *maskèd... discloses* reveals their hidden flowers (i.e., when the buds open) 9 *for* because; *virtue* excellence; *show* appearance 10 *unrespected* ignored 11 *to themselves* alone, by themselves 14 *vade* (1) depart, (2) wither; *by... truth* through (my) verse your truth is concentrated into its essence

55

Not marble nor the gilded monuments
2 Of princes shall outlive this powerful rhyme,
3 But you shall shine more bright in these contents
4 Than unswept stone, besmeared with sluttish time.
5 When wasteful war shall statues overturn,
6 And broils root out the work of masonry,
7 Nor Mars his sword nor war's quick fire shall burn
The living record of your memory.
9 'Gainst death and all oblivious enmity
10 Shall you pace forth; your praise shall still find room
Even in the eyes of all posterity
12 That wear this world out to the ending doom.
13   So, till the judgment that yourself arise,
14   You live in this, and dwell in lovers' eyes.

---

2 *this . . . rhyme* (1) this poem, (2) my poetry 3 *these contents* what is contained here 4 *Than* than you will in; *stone* (e.g., a funeral monument); *sluttish* (1) slovenly, (2) whorish 5 *wasteful* destructive 6 *broils* battles 7 *Nor . . . sword* neither Mars's sword; *quick* (1) swift, (2) living 9 *all . . . enmity* (1) cosmic enmity, which consigns everything to oblivion, (2) oblivion, which is the enemy of everything 10 *still . . . room* always find a place 12 *wear . . . doom* endure until doomsday 13 *the . . . that* Judgment Day, when 14 *dwell in* i.e., permanently inhabit

56

Sweet love, renew thy force; be it not said   1
Thy edge should blunter be than appetite,   2
Which but today by feeding is allayed,   3
Tomorrow sharpened in his former might.   4
So, love, be thou: although today thou fill
Thy hungry eyes even till they wink with fullness,   6
Tomorrow see again, and do not kill
The spirit of love with a perpetual dullness.
Let this sad interim like the ocean be   9
Which parts the shore where two contracted new   10
Come daily to the banks, that, when they see
Return of love, more blessed may be the view;
   As call it winter, which, being full of care,   13
   Makes summer's welcome thrice more wished, more rare.

---

1 *love* (the passion, not the lover) 2 *should . . . be* is less keen; *appetite* (1)
sexual desire, (2) hunger 3 *but* only 4 *sharpened . . . his* sharpened to its
6 *wink* close 9 *sad interim* unhappy intermission (in our loving) 10
parts . . . shore separates the shores; *two . . . new* a newly betrothed couple
13 *As* equally appropriately

57

1 Being your slave, what should I do but tend
 Upon the hours and times of your desire?
 I have no precious time at all to spend,
 Nor services to do till you require.
5 Nor dare I chide the world-without-end hour
 Whilst I, my sovereign, watch the clock for you,
 Nor think the bitterness of absence sour
 When you have bid your servant once adieu.
9 Nor dare I question with my jealous thought
10 Where you may be, or your affairs suppose,
 But, like a sad slave, stay and think of nought
12 Save where you are how happy you make those.
  So true a fool is love that in your will
  Though you do anything, he thinks no ill.

---

1 *tend* wait 5 *world-without-end* endless 9 *question* (1) demand to know,
(2) argue 10 *suppose* speculate about 12 *where . . . those* how happy you
make those who are where you are

58

That god forbid that made me first your slave
I should in thought control your times of pleasure,　　2
Or at your hand th' account of hours to crave,　　3
Being your vassal bound to stay your leisure.　　4
O, let me suffer, being at your beck,　　5
Th' imprisoned absence of your liberty;　　6
And patience, tame to sufferance, bide each check　　7
Without accusing you of injury.
Be where you list; your charter is so strong　　9
That you yourself may privilege your time　　10
To what you will; to you it doth belong
Yourself to pardon of self-doing crime.　　12
　I am to wait, though waiting so be hell,
　　Not blame your pleasure, be it ill or well.

---

2 *in thought* even in thought 3 *at . . . crave* i.e., demand an accounting from you of how you spend your time 4 *stay* await 5 *suffer* (1) endure, (2) allow; *beck* summons (as in "beck and call") 6 *Th' imprisoned . . . liberty* i.e., your absence, the exercise of your liberty, is imprisonment for me; *liberty* (1) freedom, (2) libertinism, licentiousness 7 *patience . . . sufferance* (1) let patience, inured to suffering, (2) let patience, tame to the point of submission; *bide . . . check* endure every rebuke 9 *list* wish; *charter* entitlement 10 *privilege* dispose of, authorize 12 *self-doing crime* offenses committed against yourself

59

1   If there be nothing new, but that which is
    Hath been before, how are our brains beguiled,
3   Which, laboring for invention, bear amiss
4   The second burden of a former child!
5   O that record could with a backward look,
6   Even of five hundred courses of the sun,
    Show me your image in some antique book,
8   Since mind at first in character was done,
    That I might see what the old world could say
10 To this composèd wonder of your frame;
11 Whether we are mended, or whe'r better they,
12 Or whether revolution be the same.
        O, sure I am the wits of former days
        To subjects worse have given admiring praise.

---

1 *that . . . is* whatever now exists   3 *invention* poetic inspiration; *bear amiss*
miscarry   4 *burden* birth; *former child* i.e., one already born   5 *record* mem-
ory (accented on the second syllable)   6 *courses . . . sun* years   8 *Since . . .*
character from the time when thought was first expressed in writing   10
To . . . wonder about this wonderful composition; *frame* form   11 *we . . .*
mended we have improved; *whe'r* whether   12 *revolution . . . same* i.e., every
cycle repeats the previous ones

60

Like as the waves make towards the pebbled shore,
So do our minutes hasten to their end;
Each changing place with that which goes before,
In sequent toil all forwards do contend.   4

Nativity, once in the main of light,   5
Crawls to maturity, wherewith being crowned,
Crooked eclipses 'gainst his glory fight,   7
And Time that gave doth now his gift confound.   8

Time doth transfix the flourish set on youth   9
And delves the parallels in beauty's brow,   10
Feeds on the rarities of nature's truth,   11
And nothing stands but for his scythe to mow:

    And yet to times in hope my verse shall stand,   13
    Praising thy worth, despite his cruel hand.

---

4 *sequent toil* successive effort; *contend* struggle 5 *Nativity* the newborn child; *the . . . light* full sun 7 *Crooked* ominous, malignant 8 *confound* destroy 9 *transfix* pierce; *flourish* bloom 10 *delves . . . parallels* digs the trenches 11 *rarities* precious things; *truth* perfection 13 *times in hope* hoped-for future times; *stand* endure

61

Is it thy will thy image should keep open
My heavy eyelids to the weary night?
Dost thou desire my slumbers should be broken
4 While shadows like to thee do mock my sight?
Is it thy spirit that thou send'st from thee
So far from home into my deeds to pry,
7 To find out shames and idle hours in me,
8 The scope and tenure of thy jealousy?
O no, thy love, though much, is not so great;
10 It is my love that keeps mine eye awake,
Mine own true love that doth my rest defeat
To play the watchman ever for thy sake.
13   For thee watch I whilst thou dost wake elsewhere,
From me far off, with others all too near.

---

4 *shadows* (1) images, (2) spirits 7 *shames* shameful behavior; *idle hours* wasted time 8 *scope . . . tenure* aim and purport, entire point; *jealousy* suspicion (the metaphor is of a landlord spying on his tenant) 13 *watch* lie awake

62

Sin of self-love possesseth all mine eye
And all my soul and all my every part;
And for this sin there is no remedy,
It is so grounded inward in my heart.   4
Methinks no face so gracious is as mine,   5
No shape so true, no truth of such account,   6
And for myself mine own worth do define
As I all other in all worths surmount.   8
But when my glass shows me myself indeed,
Beated and chopped with tanned antiquity,   10
Mine own self-love quite contrary I read;   11
Self so self-loving were iniquity:
    'Tis thee (my self) that for myself I praise,   13
    Painting my age with beauty of thy days.

---

4 *inward* in the deepest part   5 *gracious* attractive   6 *shape so true* body so
perfect; *truth* (1) honesty, (2) fidelity; *of . . . account* so praiseworthy   8 *As*
(1) since, (2) as if; *other* others; *surmount* surpass   10 *Beated* battered;
chopped chapped, wrinkled; *tanned antiquity* leathery old age   11 *contrary*
differently   13 *thee (my self)* you, my other self, or my essence; *for myself*
i.e., when I praise myself

63

1 Against my love shall be as I am now,
2 With Time's injurious hand crushed and o'erworn;
  When hours have drained his blood and filled his brow
  With lines and wrinkles, when his youthful morn
5 Hath travailed on to age's steepy night,
  And all those beauties whereof now he's king
  Are vanishing, or vanished out of sight,
  Stealing away the treasure of his spring:
9 For such a time do I now fortify
10 Against confounding age's cruel knife,
11 That he shall never cut from memory
12 My sweet love's beauty, though my lover's life.
   His beauty shall in these black lines be seen,
14   And they shall live, and he in them still green.

---

1 *Against* in anticipation of the time when   2 *crushed . . . o'erworn* crumpled
and worn out   5 *travailed* (1) labored, (2) journeyed (Elizabethan "travail"
represented both modern "travail" and "travel")   9 *fortify* build defenses   10
confounding destroying   11 *That* so that   12 *though* i.e., even though he
cuts off   14 *still green* ever young, always flourishing

64

When I have seen by Time's fell hand defaced   1
The rich proud cost of outworn buried age,   2
When sometime lofty towers I see down-razed   3
And brass eternal slave to mortal rage;   4
When I have seen the hungry ocean gain   5
Advantage on the kingdom of the shore,
And the firm soil win of the wat'ry main,
Increasing store with loss and loss with store;   8
When I have seen such interchange of state,   9
Or state itself confounded to decay,   10
Ruin hath taught me thus to ruminate,
That Time will come and take my love away.   12
   This thought is as a death, which cannot choose
   But weep to have that which it fears to lose.   14

1 *fell* cruel   2 *cost* (1) extravagance, (2) expensive objects; *outworn* worn-out 3 *sometime* formerly; *down-razed* demolished   4 *brass . . . slave* (1) everlasting brass a slave, (2) brass the eternal slave; *mortal rage* (1) deadly violence, (2) human fury, (3) the violence of death   5–6 *gain . . . on* i.e., occupy the territory of   8 *Increasing . . . with store* i.e., one gaining by the other's loss, one losing to the other's gain   9 *state* greatness   10 *confounded to* devastated to a point of   12 *love* beloved   14 *to have* for having

65

1 Since brass, nor stone, nor earth, nor boundless sea,
But sad mortality o'ersways their power,
3 How with this rage shall beauty hold a plea,
4 Whose action is no stronger than a flower?
O, how shall summer's honey breath hold out
6 Against the wrackful siege of battering days,
When rocks impregnable are not so stout,
8 Nor gates of steel so strong but time decays?
O fearful meditation: where, alack,
10 Shall Time's best jewel from Time's chest lie hid?
Or what strong hand can hold his swift foot back,
12 Or who his spoil of beauty can forbid?
        O, none, unless this miracle have might,
        That in black ink my love may still shine bright.

---

1 *Since* since there is neither 3 *hold a plea* plead its case 4 *action* (1) lawsuit, (2) power, ability to act 6 *wrackful* destructive 8 *decays* i.e., decays the *rocks* and *gates* 10 *Time's best . . . hid* the most precious jewel of the time be hidden to avoid incarceration in Time's strongbox 12 *spoil* despoiling

66

Tired with all these, for restful death I cry: 1
As, to behold desert a beggar born,   2
And needy nothing trimmed in jollity,   3
And purest faith unhappily forsworn,   4
And gilded honor shamefully misplaced,   5
And maiden virtue rudely strumpeted,   6
And right perfection wrongfully disgraced,   7
And strength by limping sway disablèd,   8
And art made tongue-tied by authority,   9
And folly (doctorlike) controlling skill,   10
And simple truth miscalled simplicity,   11
And captive good attending captain ill.   12
    Tired with all these, from these would I be gone,
    Save that, to die, I leave my love alone.

---

1 *Tired . . . these* wearied by the following things 2 *As* such as; *desert* a deserving person 3 *needy . . . jollity* a worthless nobody adorned with finery 4 *faith . . . forsworn* (1) religious belief unwillingly repudiated, (2) honesty maliciously betrayed, (3) fidelity scornfully abandoned (or any combination of these) 5 *gilded honor* rich nobility; *misplaced* wrongfully bestowed 6 *strumpeted* prostituted 7 *right* true, genuine; *disgraced* (1) slandered, (2) banished from favor 8 *by . . . disablèd* i.e., weakened by incompetent leadership 9 *art* learning, science, literature; *made . . . authority* (1) silenced by the force of tradition, (2) inhibited by those in power, censored 10 *doctorlike* as if learned, posing as an expert; *controlling skill* i.e., having authority over real talent 11 *simple* (1) plain, (2) innocent; *simplicity* stupidity 12 *attending* the servant of

67

1 Ah, wherefore with infection should he live
2 And with his presence grace impiety,
3 That sin by him advantage should achieve
4 And lace itself with his society?
5 Why should false painting imitate his cheek
6 And steal dead seeing of his living hue?
7 Why should poor beauty indirectly seek
8 Roses of shadow, since his rose is true?
  Why should he live, now Nature bankrupt is,
10 Beggared of blood to blush through lively veins,
11 For she hath no exchequer now but his,
12 And, proud of many, lives upon his gains?
13   O, him she stores, to show what wealth she had
14   In days long since, before these last so bad.

---

1 *wherefore* why; *with infection* i.e., in a corrupt world   2 *grace* adorn   3 *advantage* benefit   4 *lace* (1) adorn, (2) thoroughly infuse (cf. "lace with brandy"), (3) girdle   5 *false painting* i.e., those who use cosmetics   6 *dead seeing* the lifeless appearance   7 *poor* inferior; *indirectly* (1) by indirection, dishonestly, (2) through artifice   8 *Roses of shadow* merely to look like roses   10 *Beggared* drained   11 *exchequer* i.e., treasury of natural beauty   12 *proud . . . gains* (1) though she is justly proud of many beauties through the ages (*In days long since*, l. 14), she now lives only on the beauty he produces, (2) though she is proud of many beauties, only his provides her with real sustenance   13 *stores* preserves   14 *last* most recent days

68

Thus is his cheek the map of days outworn   1
When beauty lived and died as flowers do now,
Before these bastard signs of fair were born   3
Or durst inhabit on a living brow;   4
Before the golden tresses of the dead,
The right of sepulchres, were shorn away   6
To live a second life on second head,
Ere beauty's dead fleece made another gay: 8
In him those holy antique hours are seen,   9
Without all ornament, itself and true,   10
Making no summer of another's green,
Robbing no old to dress his beauty new;
　　And him as for a map doth Nature store,   13
　　To show false Art what beauty was of yore.

---

1 *map* depiction; *days outworn* past times 3 *bastard . . . fair* illegitimate
marks of beauty – i.e., cosmetics; *born* (1) invented, (2) (*borne*) worn 4 *in-
habit* dwell 6 *The right of* properly belonging to 8 *fleece* hair; *gay* (1)
pretty, (2) flashily attractive 9 *antique hours* ancient times 10 *itself . . .
true* its essential self 13 *map* guide; *store* preserve

69

1 Those parts of thee that the world's eye doth view
2 Want nothing that the thought of hearts can mend;
3 All tongues, the voice of souls, give thee that due,
4 Utt'ring bare truth, even so as foes commend.
5 Thy outward thus with outward praise is crowned,
6 But those same tongues that give thee so thine own
7 In other accents do this praise confound
  By seeing farther than the eye hath shown.
  They look into the beauty of thy mind,
10 And that in guess they measure by thy deeds;
  Then, churls, their thoughts, although their eyes were kind,
12 To thy fair flower add the rank smell of weeds:
  But why thy odor matcheth not thy show,
14 The soil is this, that thou dost common grow.

---

1 *parts* (1) physical attributes, (2) excellent qualities 2 *Want* lack; *thought of hearts* (1) deepest thoughts, (2) strongest desires; *mend* improve 3 *the . . . souls* i.e., heartfelt utterances 4 *bare* simple, straightforward; *even . . . commend* in the way that one's enemies praise one (i.e., grudgingly) 5 *Thy outward* your external qualities 6 *thine own* what is your due 7 *confound* (1) contradict, (2) destroy 10 *in guess* by guessing 12 *add . . . weeds* i.e., soil your reputation, "put you in bad odor" 14 *soil* (1) ground, (2) explanation, (3) blot, stain; *common* commonplace, vulgar

70

That thou art blamed shall not be thy defect,   1
For slander's mark was ever yet the fair;   2
The ornament of beauty is suspect,   3
A crow that flies in heaven's sweetest air.
So thou be good, slander doth but approve   5
Thy worth the greater, being wooed of time;   6
For canker vice the sweetest buds doth love,   7
And thou present'st a pure unstainèd prime.   8
Thou hast passed by the ambush of young days,   9
Either not assailed, or victor being charged;   10
Yet this thy praise cannot be so thy praise   11
To tie up envy, evermore enlarged: 12
    If some suspect of ill masked not thy show,   13
    Then thou alone kingdoms of hearts shouldst owe.   14

---

1 *thy defect* a fault in you, something to hold against you 2 *mark* target 3 *ornament* adornment, reward; *suspect* suspicion 5 *So* so long as; *approve* prove 6 *wooed of time* (1) showered with the gifts of the time, (2) tempted by the (vices of the) age (and not yielding) 7 *canker vice* vice, like a cankerworm 8 *prime* youth 9 *ambush . . . days* traps laid for youth 10 *charged* attacked 11 *so* so much 12 *To* as to; *evermore enlarged* always being released 13 *some . . . show* some suspicion of evil did not falsely cover you 14 *owe* own

71

No longer mourn for me when I am dead
Than you shall hear the surly sullen bell
Give warning to the world that I am fled
From this vile world, with vilest worms to dwell.
Nay, if you read this line, remember not
The hand that writ it, for I love you so
That I in your sweet thoughts would be forgot
8 If thinking on me then should make you woe.
O, if, I say, you look upon this verse
10 When I, perhaps, compounded am with clay,
11 Do not so much as my poor name rehearse,
But let your love even with my life decay,
Lest the wise world should look into your moan
14 And mock you with me after I am gone.

---

8 *make . . . woe* cause you grief   11 *rehearse* repeat   14 *with me* as it mocks
me

72

O, lest the world should task you to recite   1
What merit lived in me that you should love
After my death, dear love, forget me quite,
For you in me can nothing worthy prove;   4
Unless you would devise some virtuous lie,   5
To do more for me than mine own desert
And hang more praise upon deceasèd I   7
Than niggard truth would willingly impart.   8
O, lest your true love may seem false in this,   9
That you for love speak well of me untrue,   10
My name be buried where my body is,   11
And live no more to shame nor me nor you;   12
    For I am shamed by that which I bring forth   13
    And so should you, to love things nothing worth.   14

---

1 *task you* (1) require you, (2) challenge you   4 *prove* show   5 *virtuous* (1) potent, (2) generous   7 *hang* . . . *I* (the image is of trophies hung on a tomb; grammatically, *I* should be "me")   8 *niggard* the miser   9 *false* (1) dishonest, (2) unfaithful   10 *untrue* untruthfully   11 *My name* let my name   12 *nor* . . . *nor* neither . . . nor   13 *that* . . . *forth* (depending on how autobiographical one wishes the sonnets to be, the reference can be a narrow one to poems such as this or a much broader one to Shakespeare's work as a popular playwright)   14 *should you* you too would be

73

That time of year thou mayst in me behold
When yellow leaves, or none, or few, do hang
Upon those boughs which shake against the cold,
4 Bare ruined choirs where late the sweet birds sang.
In me thou seest the twilight of such day
As after sunset fadeth in the west,
Which by and by black night doth take away,
8 Death's second self that seals up all in rest.
In me thou seest the glowing of such fire
10 That on the ashes of his youth doth lie,
As the deathbed whereon it must expire,
Consumed with that which it was nourished by.
    This thou perceiv'st, which makes thy love more strong,
14   To love that well which thou must leave ere long.

---

4 *ruined choirs* (the choir is the part of the church behind the altar, in which
the choir sings; ruined choirs were a commonplace sight in England after the
destruction of the monasteries during Henry VIII's reign); *sweet birds* (1)
songbirds driven off by winter, (2) choristers driven away by the Protestant
Reformation   8 *seals up* (1) encloses as in a coffin, (2) puts the seal on a doc-
ument, (3) seels up – i.e., stitches closed the eyes of a hawk   14 *leave* (1) de-
part from, (2) give up

74

But be contented when that fell arrest   1
Without all bail shall carry me away,   2
My life hath in this line some interest   3
Which for memorial still with thee shall stay.   4
When thou reviewest this, thou dost review   5
The very part was consecrate to thee: 6
The earth can have but earth, which is his due;   7
My spirit is thine, the better part of me.
So then thou hast but lost the dregs of life,
The prey of worms, my body being dead,   10
The coward conquest of a wretch's knife,   11
Too base of thee to be rememberèd.   12
    The worth of that is that which it contains,   13
    And that is this, and this with thee remains.   14

---

1 *fell* cruel 2 *Without . . . bail* i.e., with no possibility of release 3 *in . . . interest* some rights persisting in these lines (the poem, reduced to a *line*, is considered as a piece of property or an estate) 4 *memorial* (1) a monument, (2) a memorandum; *still* (1) always, (2) nevertheless 5 *reviewest* reread; *review* see again 6 *very part* (the *better part*, l. 8); *was consecrate* that was devoted 7 *his* its 11 *The . . . knife* (a much debated line; the *wretch* is most plausibly explained as Death, and the speaker is cowardly for yielding to him) 12 *of* by 13 *The . . . contains* the value of the body is the spirit within it 14 *that is this* i.e., my spirit animates this poem

75

So are you to my thoughts as food to life,
2   Or as sweet-seasoned showers are to the ground;
3   And for the peace of you I hold such strife
    As 'twixt a miser and his wealth is found:
5   Now proud as an enjoyer, and anon
6   Doubting the filching age will steal his treasure;
7   Now counting best to be with you alone,
8   Then bettered that the world may see my pleasure;
    Sometime all full with feasting on your sight,
10 And by and by clean starvèd for a look,
    Possessing or pursuing no delight
12 Save what is had or must from you be took.
13   Thus do I pine and surfeit day by day,
14   Or gluttoning on all, or all away.

---

2 *sweet-seasoned* (1) sweetly flavored, (2) springtime 3 *for . . . you* (1) be-
cause of the peace you bring me, (2) in order to obtain the peace you would
bring me, (3) instead of the peace you represent for me; *hold . . . strife* i.e.,
am in just such tension 5 *Now . . . anon* at first delighting in my possession,
and soon after 6 *Doubting* fearing, suspecting 7 *counting* accounting it,
considering it 8 *bettered* better pleased 10 *clean* absolutely 12 *must . . .
took* can only be received from you 13 *pine* (1) starve, (2) yearn 14 *Or
gluttoning* either gorging myself; *all away* finding everything gone

76

Why is my verse so barren of new pride?	1
So far from variation or quick change?	2
Why, with the time, do I not glance aside	3
To new-found methods and to compounds strange?	4
Why write I still all one, ever the same,	5
And keep invention in a noted weed,	6
That every word doth almost tell my name,	7
Showing their birth, and where they did proceed?	8
O, know, sweet love, I always write of you,	
And you and love are still my argument;	10
So all my best is dressing old words new,	11
Spending again what is already spent:	12
For as the sun is daily new and old,	
So is my love still telling what is told.	14

1 *new pride* stylish ornament   2 *variation . . . change* variety and lively conceits (the terms are synonymous, not alternatives)   3 *with . . . time* as is the current fashion; *glance* turn   4 *methods* poetic techniques; *compounds strange* far-fetched metaphors or compound words   5 *still . . . one* always in one way   6 *invention* poetic creation; *noted weed* familiar dress, "the same old clothes"   7 *That* so that   8 *where . . . proceed* (1) where they came from, (2) where they went, (3) what school they graduated from   10 *argument* subject   11 *all my best* the best I can do   12 *spent* (1) paid, (2) worn out   14 *telling* (1) counting (cf. *spent*, l. 12), (2) recounting

77

1 Thy glass will show thee how thy beauties wear,
2 Thy dial how thy precious minutes waste;
3 The vacant leaves thy mind's imprint will bear,
4 And of this book this learning mayst thou taste.
  The wrinkles which thy glass will truly show,
6 Of mouthèd graves will give thee memory.
  Thou by thy dial's shady stealth mayst know
  Time's thievish progress to eternity.
9 Look what thy memory cannot contain,
10 Commit to these waste blanks, and thou shalt find
11 Those children nursed, delivered from thy brain,
  To take a new acquaintance of thy mind.
13   These offices, so oft as thou wilt look,
    Shall profit thee and much enrich thy book.

---

1 *glass* mirror; *wear* age, fade 2 *dial* sundial (see *shady*, l. 7); *waste* pass, waste away 3 *vacant leaves* blank pages (see *waste blanks*, l. 10: the poem accompanies a blank book in which the young man is to *imprint* his mind – cf. Sonnet 122) 4 *of* from; *this learning* i.e., the wisdom that follows; *taste* experience 6 *mouthèd* (and hence devouring); *give . . . memory* remind you 9 *Look what* whatever 10 *waste blanks* blank pages 11 *nursed, delivered* i.e., the ideas you have given birth to, like children who have matured past the nursing stage 13 *offices* duties; *so oft* whenever; *look* (at the *glass*, at the *book*)

78

So oft have I invoked thee for my muse
And found such fair assistance in my verse
As every alien pen hath got my use   3
And under thee their poesy disperse.   4
Thine eyes, that taught the dumb on high to sing,   5
And heavy ignorance aloft to fly,
Have added feathers to the learnèd's wing   7
And given grace a double majesty.   8
Yet be most proud of that which I compile,   9
Whose influence is thine and born of thee.   10
In others' works thou dost but mend the style   11
And arts with thy sweet graces gracèd be;
　　But thou art all my art and dost advance   13
　　As high as learning my rude ignorance.

---

3 *As* that; *every . . . pen* every other poet, poets who are complete strangers to you; *got . . . use* followed my lead   4 *under thee* with you as muse or patron; *disperse* disseminate (either by publication or by circulating it in manuscript)   5 *on high* aloud (quibbling on *aloft*, l. 6)   7 *added feathers* (in falconry, the hawk is imped, or given extra wing feathers, to enable it to fly higher; the feathers also play on the metaphor of the *pen*, which would have been a quill)   8 *given . . . majesty* made the eloquent and learned doubly great   9 *compile* compose   10 *influence* (the metaphor is astrological: the young man is the star under which the poetry is born)   11 *mend* improve   13 *advance* elevate

79

Whilst I alone did call upon thy aid,
2 My verse alone had all thy gentle grace;
3 But now my gracious numbers are decayed,
4 And my sick muse doth give another place.
5 I grant, sweet love, thy lovely argument
Deserves the travail of a worthier pen;
7 Yet what of thee thy poet doth invent
He robs thee of, and pays it thee again.
9 He lends thee virtue, and he stole that word
10 From thy behavior; beauty doth he give,
11 And found it in thy cheek: he can afford
No praise to thee but what in thee doth live.
Then thank him not for that which he doth say,
Since what he owes thee thou thyself dost pay.

---

2 *had . . . grace* (1) expressed all your aristocratic charm, (2) had all your
kind favor, (3) had all the same graciousness as you do 3 *gracious numbers*
verses imbued with your *grace* 4 *give . . . place* yield its place to another poet
5 *thy . . . argument* (1) the theme of your loveliness, (2) the lovely topic you
are 7 *of thee* concerning you 9 *lends thee* credits you with 11 *afford* offer

80

O, how I faint when I of you do write, 1
Knowing a better spirit doth use your name 2
And in the praise thereof spends all his might 3
To make me tongue-tied, speaking of your fame.
But since your worth (wide as the ocean is)
The humble as the proudest sail doth bear, 6
My saucy bark, inferior far to his,
On your broad main doth willfully appear. 8
Your shallowest help will hold me up afloat 9
Whilst he upon your soundless deep doth ride; 10
Or, being wrecked, I am a worthless boat,
He of tall building and of goodly pride. 12
    Then if he thrive, and I be cast away, 13
    The worst was this: my love was my decay. 14

---

1 *faint* lose heart   2 *spirit* wit – i.e., a more gifted poet; *use . . . name* (1) dedicate his poems to you (as Shakespeare "used" the Earl of Southampton in *Venus and Adonis* and *Lucrece*), (2) write about you, (3) invoke your name as his muse   3–4 *spends . . . tongue-tied* (1) tries as hard as he can to silence me, (2) is so forceful that the result silences me (perhaps with sexual over-tones: "spend" is the term for having an orgasm)   6 *as* as well as   8 *main* ocean; *willfully* (1) boldly, (2) obstinately   9 *shallowest* slightest (with the implication that the speaker's small craft keeps safely to the shallows)   10 *soundless* unfathomable (but playing ironically on *tongue-tied*, l. 4)   12 *of . . . building* tall-masted; *goodly pride* great splendor   13 *cast away* (1) shipwrecked, (2) dismissed   14 *decay* ruin

81

1 Or I shall live your epitaph to make,
   Or you survive when I in earth am rotten,
3 From hence your memory death cannot take,
4 Although in me each part will be forgotten.
5 Your name from hence immortal life shall have,
6 Though I, once gone, to all the world must die.
   The earth can yield me but a common grave
   When you entombèd in men's eyes shall lie.
   Your monument shall be my gentle verse,
10 Which eyes not yet created shall o'erread;
11 And tongues to be your being shall rehearse
   When all the breathers of this world are dead.
13   You still shall live (such virtue hath my pen)
14   Where breath most breathes, even in the mouths of men.

---

1 *Or* whether   3 *hence* (1) this world, (2) these poems   4 *in . . . part* all my
virtues   5 *from hence* (1) henceforth, (2) from this poetry   6 *to . . . world* as
far as the world is concerned   11 *rehearse* recite   13 *virtue* power   14
breath (1) speech, (2) spirit

82

I grant thou wert not married to my muse
And therefore mayst without attaint o'erlook   2
The dedicated words which writers use   3
Of their fair subject, blessing every book.
Thou art as fair in knowledge as in hue,   5
Finding thy worth a limit past my praise;   6
And therefore art enforced to seek anew
Some fresher stamp of the time-bettering days.   8
And do so, love; yet when they have devised
What strainèd touches rhetoric can lend,   10
Thou, truly fair, wert truly sympathized   11
In true plain words by thy true-telling friend:
    And their gross painting might be better used   13
    Where cheeks need blood; in thee it is abused.   14

---

2 *attaint* dishonor, the accusation of unfaithfulness; *o'erlook* read through
3 *dedicated* (1) devoted, (2) particular to you (in works dedicated to you)
5 *hue* (1) complexion, (2) appearance   6 *Finding . . . past* (1) knowing as
you do that your virtues extend beyond, (2) knowing as I do that your
virtues extend beyond   8 *stamp* imprint (the metaphor is from printing or
from the minting of coins and medals); *time-bettering days* continually im-
proving times   10 *strainèd touches* exaggerated effects   11 *truly sympathized*
truthfully represented   13 *gross* (1) thick, (2) vulgar   14 *Where . . . blood*
i.e., on faces in need of the *painting* of cosmetics; *in thee* in your case; *abused*
misused

83

1 I never saw that you did painting need,
2 And therefore to your fair no painting set;
I found, or thought I found, you did exceed
4 The barren tender of a poet's debt:
5 And therefore have I slept in your report,
That you yourself, being extant, well might show
7 How far a modern quill doth come too short,
8 Speaking of worth, what worth in you doth grow.
9 This silence for my sin you did impute,
10 Which shall be most my glory, being dumb,
For I impair not beauty, being mute,
12 When others would give life and bring a tomb.
There lives more life in one of your fair eyes
14 Than both your poets can in praise devise.

---

1 *painting* (1) cosmetics, (2) rhetorical embellishment 2 *fair* beauty; *set* applied 4 *barren tender* worthless offering; *debt* indebtedness (to his patron) 5 *slept . . . report* been dilatory in writing of you 7 *modern quill* (1) contemporary poet, (2) commonplace writer 8 *Speaking . . . what worth* in speaking of worth (when it tries to tell) what worth 9 *for* as 12 *bring a tomb* i.e., merely create a monument to you 14 *both . . . poets* (Shakespeare and the rival poet; see Sonnets 78–80)

84

Who is it that says most, which can say more   1
Than this rich praise, that you alone are you,
In whose confine immurèd is the store   3
Which should example where your equal grew?   4
Lean penury within that pen doth dwell   5
That to his subject lends not some small glory,
But he that writes of you, if he can tell
That you are you, so dignifies his story.   8
Let him but copy what in you is writ,
Not making worse what nature made so clear,   10
And such a counterpart shall fame his wit,   11
Making his style admired everywhere.
 You to your beauteous blessings add a curse,
 Being fond on praise, which makes your praises worse.   14

1 *Who . . . more* who that praises you most can say anything more   3 *In . . . immurèd is* within whose walls is enclosed; *store* treasure   4 *should . . . grew* i.e., would have to be the benchmark for whatever nurtures your equal   5 *pen* i.e., poet (punning on *confine*, l. 3)   8 *so* thereby   10 *clear* (1) glorious, (2) perfect ("unspotted")   11 *counterpart* copy; *fame . . . wit* bring fame to his poetic skill   14 *fond on praise* (1) fond of flattery, (2) foolishly lavish with your praise

85

1 My tongue-tied muse in manners holds her still
2 While comments of your praise, richly compiled,
3 Reserve their character with golden quill
4 And precious phrase by all the muses filed.
  I think good thoughts whilst other write good words,
6 And, like unlettered clerk, still cry "Amen"
7 To every hymn that able spirit affords
8 In polished form of well-refinèd pen.
  Hearing you praised, I say, " 'Tis so, 'tis true,"
10 And to the most of praise add something more;
  But that is in my thought, whose love to you,
12 Though words come hindmost, holds his rank before.
13   Then others for the breath of words respect;
14   Me for my dumb thoughts, speaking in effect.

---

1 *in . . . still* politely remains silent 2 *comments . . . compiled* elaborately composed commentaries praising you 3 *Reserve . . . character* (probably "preserve their writings"; a much debated and emended passage) 4 *filed* polished 6 *unlettered clerk* the illiterate parish clerk (whose duty it is to lead the congregation's responses, and cries *Amen* to everything); *still* always 7 *hymn* poem of praise; *able . . . affords* capable poet provides 8 *form* style 10 *most of* utmost 12 *Though . . . before* i.e., though I rank behind other poets in singing your praise, my silent thoughts make me their superior 13 *others . . . respect* regard others for the words they speak, which are only breath 14 *in effect* (1) virtually, (2) in reality

86

Was it the proud full sail of his great verse,   1
Bound for the prize of all-too-precious you,   2
That did my ripe thoughts in my brain inhearse,   3
Making their tomb the womb wherein they grew?   4
Was it his spirit, by spirits taught to write   5
Above a mortal pitch, that struck me dead?   6
No, neither he, nor his compeers by night   7
Giving him aid, my verse astonishèd.   8
He, nor that affable familiar ghost   9
Which nightly gulls him with intelligence,   10
As victors, of my silence cannot boast;   11
I was not sick of any fear from thence: 12
    But when your countenance filled up his line,   13
    Then lacked I matter; that enfeebled mine.   14

---

1 *his* (a rival poet for the young man's patronage; not necessarily the same as the rival in Sonnets 78–80; attempts have been made on the basis of the characterization in ll. 5–8 to identify him as Shakespeare's contemporary George Chapman) 2 *prize* (the metaphor is of a privateer or pirate ship) 3 *ripe* mature, ready to be expressed; *inhearse* bury 5 *spirit* (1) wit, (2) genius, inner daemon, (3) soul; *spirits* (1) other wits, (2) supernatural inspiration 6 *Above . . . pitch* in a more elevated style than ordinary mortals use; *pitch* height (the metaphor is from falconry); *struck . . . dead* silenced me, "knocked me out" 7 *his compeers . . . night* those nocturnal spirits (whether supernatural or intellectual) whom he consults 8 *astonishèd* astounded, stunned 9 *He* neither he; *that . . . ghost* his genial familiar spirit 10 *gulls . . . intelligence* (1) crams him full of news, (2) deceives him with rumors 11 *of . . . boast* cannot claim that they have silenced me 13 *countenance* (1) face, (2) approval; *line* verse 14 *matter* subject matter

87

1 Farewell, thou art too dear for my possessing,
2 And like enough thou know'st thy estimate.
3 The charter of thy worth gives thee releasing;
4 My bonds in thee are all determinate.
  For how do I hold thee but by thy granting,
6 And for that riches where is my deserving?
7 The cause of this fair gift in me is wanting,
8 And so my patent back again is swerving.
  Thyself thou gav'st, thy own worth then not knowing,
10 Or me, to whom thou gav'st it, else mistaking;
11 So thy great gift, upon misprision growing,
12 Comes home again, on better judgment making.
    Thus have I had thee as a dream doth flatter,
    In sleep a king, but waking no such matter.

---

1 *dear* (1) precious, (2) expensive 2 *estimate* value 3 *charter* privilege (the metaphor is of a legal document, like a *patent,* conferring value); *gives . . . releasing* releases you from obligation 4 *bonds in* claims on; *determinate* ended 6 *riches* wealth (not a plural) 7 *cause of* justification for; *wanting* lacking 8 *patent* exclusive right (to your love); *back . . . swerving* i.e., reverts to you 10 *mistaking* misjudging 11 *upon . . . growing* based on error 12 *on . . . making* as you arrive at a better judgment

88

When thou shalt be disposed to set me light,   1
And place my merit in the eye of scorn,   2
Upon thy side against myself I'll fight
And prove thee virtuous, though thou art forsworn.   4
With mine own weakness being best acquainted,
Upon thy part I can set down a story   6
Of faults concealed wherein I am attainted,   7
That thou, in losing me, shall win much glory;   8
And I by this will be a gainer too:
For, bending all my loving thoughts on thee   10
The injuries that to myself I do,
Doing thee vantage, double-vantage me.   12
    Such is my love, to thee I so belong,
    That for thy right myself will bear all wrong.   14

---

1 *set . . . light* hold me cheap 2 *place . . . scorn* (1) regard my worth with a scornful eye, (2) hold my worth up to ridicule 4 *art forsworn* have perjured yourself, have betrayed your trust 6 *Upon . . . part* taking your side 7 *wherein . . . attainted* of which I am guilty 8 *That* so that 10 *bending* turning 12 *vantage* benefit 14 *for . . . right* (1) to put you in the right, (2) to maintain your privilege

89

Say that thou didst forsake me for some fault,
2 And I will comment upon that offense;
3 Speak of my lameness, and I straight will halt,
4 Against thy reasons making no defense.
5 Thou canst not, love, disgrace me half so ill,
6 To set a form upon desirèd change,
7 As I'll my self disgrace, knowing thy will:
8 I will acquaintance strangle and look strange,
9 Be absent from thy walks, and in my tongue
10 Thy sweet belovèd name no more shall dwell,
11 Lest I, too much profane, should do it wrong
12 And haply of our old acquaintance tell.
13   For thee, against my self I'll vow debate,
    For I must ne'er love him whom thou dost hate.

---

2 *comment upon* expatiate, write a commentary on 3 *Speak ... lameness*
claim that I am lame; *straight* immediately; *halt* limp 4 *reasons* charges 5
disgrace (1) shame, (2) remove from favor; *ill* badly 6 *To ... upon* in giving
a shape to; *desirèd change* i.e., the change you desire in our relationship 7
thy will what you wish 8 *acquaintance strangle* kill off our friendship, deny
any acquaintance with you; *look strange* act like a stranger 9 *Be ... walks*
avoid the places where you walk 11 *profane* blaspheming 12 *haply* (1) per-
haps, (2) by chance 13 *vow debate* declare war

90

Then hate me when thou wilt, if ever, now,
Now, while the world is bent my deeds to cross,   2
Join with the spite of fortune, make me bow,   3
And do not drop in for an afterloss.   4
Ah, do not, when my heart hath scaped this sorrow,   5
Come in the rearward of a conquered woe;   6
Give not a windy night a rainy morrow,
To linger out a purposed overthrow.   8
If thou wilt leave me, do not leave me last,
When other petty griefs have done their spite,   10
But in the onset come: so shall I taste   11
At first the very worst of fortune's might;
    And other strains of woe, which now seem woe,   13
    Compared with loss of thee will not seem so.

2 *bent . . . cross* determined to thwart whatever I do   3 *bow* submit, surren-
der   4 *drop . . . afterloss* descend on me, crush me, after I am already de-
feated   5 *scaped* escaped   6 *Come . . . woe* like a rear guard, attack a grief
already conquered   8 *To . . . overthrow* in order to prolong the defeat you
(and *fortune*) have planned   11 *in . . . onset* among the first   13 *strains* (1)
kinds, (2) stresses

91

1 Some glory in their birth, some in their skill,
2 Some in their wealth, some in their body's force,
3 Some in their garments, though newfangled ill,
4 Some in their hawks and hounds, some in their horse;
5 And every humor hath his adjunct pleasure,
  Wherein it finds a joy above the rest,
7 But these particulars are not my measure;
8 All these I better in one general best.
  Thy love is better than high birth to me,
10 Richer than wealth, prouder than garments' cost,
  Of more delight than hawks or horses be;
12 And having thee, of all men's pride I boast:
    Wretched in this alone, that thou mayst take
    All this away and me most wretched make.

---

1 *skill* knowledge, wit, intellectual prowess 2 *force* strength 3 *newfangled
ill* badly styled in the newest fashion 4 *horse* horses 5 *humor . . . pleasure*
disposition has its own particular kind of enjoyment 7 *my measure* suffi-
cient or appropriate for me 8 *better* improve upon 12 *all . . . pride* every-
thing men take pride in

92

But do thy worst to steal thyself away,   1
For term of life thou art assurèd mine,   2
And life no longer than thy love will stay, ·
For it depends upon that love of thine.
Then need I not to fear the worst of wrongs   5
When in the least of them my life hath end;   6
I see a better state to me belongs
Than that which on thy humor doth depend.   8
Thou canst not vex me with inconstant mind,   9
Since that my life on thy revolt doth lie.   10
O, what a happy title do I find,   11
Happy to have thy love, happy to die!
    But what's so blessèd fair that fears no blot?   13
    Thou mayst be false, and yet I know it not.

---

1 *steal . . . away* i.e., rob me of you 2 *term of life* my lifetime 5 *worst . . . wrongs* i.e., the loss of your love 6 *the . . . them* i.e., the least sign of coldness 8 *humor* (1) mood, (2) whim, (3) character 9 *with . . . mind* by being unfaithful 10 *on . . . lie* is determined by your inconstancy 11 *happy title* lucky right, fortunate possession 13 *blessèd fair* fortunate and beautiful

93

So shall I live, supposing thou art true,
2 Like a deceivèd husband; so love's face
3 May still seem love to me though altered new,
Thy looks with me, thy heart in other place.
For there can live no hatred in thine eye;
Therefore in that I cannot know thy change;
In many's looks the false heart's history
8 Is writ in moods and frowns and wrinkles strange:
But heaven in thy creation did decree
10 That in thy face sweet love should ever dwell;
Whate'er thy thoughts or thy heart's workings be,
Thy looks should nothing thence but sweetness tell.
    How like Eve's apple doth thy beauty grow
14   If thy sweet virtue answer not thy show!

---

2 *love's face* the mere appearance of love 3 *altered new* newly changed
8 *moods* moodiness; *strange* (1) unfriendly, (2) unfamiliar 14 *virtue* (1)
character, (2) manly force, (3) goodness, (4) chastity; *answer . . . show* does
not correspond to your looks

94

They that have power to hurt and will do none,   1
That do not do the thing they most do show,   2
Who, moving others, are themselves as stone,
Unmovèd, cold, and to temptation slow –   4
They rightly do inherit heaven's graces
And husband nature's riches from expense;   6
They are the lords and owners of their faces,   7
Others but stewards of their excellence.   8
The summer's flower is to the summer sweet,
Though to itself it only live and die;   10
But if that flower with base infection meet,
The basest weed outbraves his dignity: 12
    For sweetest things turn sourest by their deeds;   13
    Lilies that fester smell far worse than weeds.   14

---

1 *They . . . none* (proverbial: "To be able to do harm and not to do it is noble") 2 *most do show* (1) appear most able to do, (2) are expected to do 4 *to . . . slow* not easily tempted (an unquestionable virtue, unlike the ambiguous *Unmovèd, cold*) 6 *husband . . . expense* i.e., preserve the bounty nature has endowed them with from dissipation 7 *lords . . . owners* sole possessors, in complete control; *of . . . faces* i.e., of how the world sees them 8 *stewards* caretakers, managers (the steward was the chief domestic officer in an aristocratic household); *their* (1) the *lords and owners'*, (2) the *stewards'* own 10 *to itself* (1) for itself, (2) by itself (without procreating) 12 *outbraves . . . dignity* surpasses its (1) excellence, (2) high rank 13 *by . . . deeds* i.e., through their own actions (the *flower* characterized by its total passivity now becomes responsible for its own corruption – this is paradoxical as a statement about the flower, but it leads back to the idealized passive figures of the opening, and suggests a world of negative possibilities for them) 14 *Lilies . . . weeds* (proverbial wisdom; the line appears verbatim in the anonymous play *Edward III*, published 1596, sometimes ascribed to Shakespeare)

95

How sweet and lovely dost thou make the shame
2 Which, like a canker in the fragrant rose,
3 Doth spot the beauty of thy budding name!
4 O, in what sweets dost thou thy sins enclose!
That tongue that tells the story of thy days,
6 Making lascivious comments on thy sport,
Cannot dispraise, but in a kind of praise,
Naming thy name, blesses an ill report.
O, what a mansion have those vices got
10 Which for their habitation chose out thee,
Where beauty's veil doth cover every blot
And all things turns to fair that eyes can see!
13 Take heed, dear heart, of this large privilege;
14 The hardest knife ill used doth lose his edge.

---

2 *canker* cankerworm, caterpillar 3 *name* reputation 4 *sweets* (1) sweet-
ness, (2) pleasures, especially sexual 6 *sport* sexual adventures 13 *Take
heed* beware 14 *his* its

96

Some say thy fault is youth, some wantonness;   1
Some say thy grace is youth and gentle sport;   2
Both grace and faults are loved of more and less: 3
Thou mak'st faults graces that to thee resort.   4
As on the finger of a thronèd queen
The basest jewel will be well esteemed,
So are those errors that in thee are seen
To truths translated and for true things deemed.   8
How many lambs might the stern wolf betray   9
If like a lamb he could his looks translate!   10
How many gazers mightst thou lead away   11
If thou wouldst use the strength of all thy state!   12
    But do not so; I love thee in such sort   13
    As, thou being mine, mine is thy good report.   14

---

1 *wantonness* (1) high spirits, (2) lechery, (3) flippancy, irresponsibility 2 *gentle* aristocratic 3 *of . . . less* by high and low, people of all classes 4 *Thou mak'st . . . resort* you turn the faults that flock to you into graces 8 *To . . . deemed* transformed into virtues and duly considered virtues 9 *stern* cruel 10 *his . . . translate* change his appearance 11 *gazers* admirers; *away* astray 12 *strength . . . state* full force of your status; *state* (1) nature (including both appearance and personality), (2) high rank 13–14 *But . . . report* (the same couplet concludes Sonnet 36) 13 *in . . . sort* in such a way 14 *report* reputation

97

How like a winter hath my absence been
From thee, the pleasure of the fleeting year!
What freezings have I felt, what dark days seen!
What old December's bareness everywhere!
5 And yet this time removed was summer's time,
6 The teeming autumn, big with rich increase,
7 Bearing the wanton burden of the prime,
8 Like widowed wombs after their lords' decease:
9 Yet this abundant issue seemed to me
10 But hope of orphans and unfathered fruit;
11 For summer and his pleasures wait on thee,
12 And, thou away, the very birds are mute;
13   Or, if they sing, 'tis with so dull a cheer
        That leaves look pale, dreading the winter's near.

---

5 *this . . . removed* in fact, the time of my absence   6 *teeming* fertile; *rich increase* numerous offspring (i.e., prolific harvests)   7 *Bearing . . . prime* pregnant with the progeny of lecherous springtime; *wanton* (1) untrammeled, (2) lascivious, (3) sportive; *prime* spring   8 *lords'* husbands'   9 *issue* offspring (yet to be born)   10 *But . . . orphans* merely the promise of orphans (since you, the father, are absent)   11 *his* its; *wait on* attend, serve   12 *thou away* since you are gone   13 *so . . . cheer* so disconsolately

98

From you have I been absent in the spring,
When proud-pied April, dressed in all his trim,   2
Hath put a spirit of youth in every thing,
That heavy Saturn laughed and leapt with him;   4
Yet nor the lays of birds, nor the sweet smell   5
Of different flowers in odor and in hue,   6
Could make me any summer's story tell,   7
Or from their proud lap pluck them where they grew;   8
Nor did I wonder at the lily's white,
Nor praise the deep vermilion in the rose;   10
They were but sweet, but figures of delight,   11
Drawn after you, you pattern of all those.   12
    Yet seemed it winter still, and you away,
    As with your shadow I with these did play.   14

2 *proud-pied* splendidly dappled; *trim* finery 4 *Saturn* (the most distant, and therefore the slowest and coldest, planet, astrologically controlling the melancholic humor) 5 *nor . . . lays* neither the songs 6 *different flowers* flowers differing 7 *summer's* i.e., cheerful 8 *proud lap* splendid earth 11 *figures of* metaphors for, representations of 12 *Drawn after* copies of 14 *shadow* image, picture

99

1 The forward violet thus did I chide:
2 Sweet thief, whence didst thou steal thy sweet that smells,
3 If not from my love's breath? The purple pride
4 Which on thy soft cheek for complexion dwells
5 In my love's veins thou hast too grossly dyed.
6 The lily I condemnèd for thy hand;
7 And buds of marjoram had stol'n thy hair;
8 The roses fearfully on thorns did stand,
   One blushing shame, another white despair;
10 A third, nor red nor white, had stol'n of both,
11 And to his robb'ry had annexed thy breath;
   But, for his theft, in pride of all his growth
13 A vengeful canker ate him up to death.
    More flowers I noted, yet I none could see
15   But sweet or color it had stol'n from thee.

The only fifteen-line sonnet in the volume.
1 *forward* (1) early-flowering, (2) presumptuous 2 *thy . . . smells* your sweet odor 3 *purple* (anything from crimson to lavender and blue, with connotations of royal magnificence); *pride* splendor 4 *complexion* color 5 *grossly* obviously, vulgarly 6 *for . . . hand* i.e., for stealing its whiteness from your hand (the lover is now being addressed) 7 *marjoram* (presumably invoked because of its sweet smell) 8 *fearfully* i.e., guiltily 10 *nor . . . white* neither red nor white, but pink or damasked (and thus brazenly feeling neither shame nor despair – since the theft is from the previous two roses, this one would be a hybrid) 11 *annexed* added the theft of 13 *canker* cankerworm, caterpillar 15 *sweet* perfume

100

Where art thou, muse, that thou forget'st so long
To speak of that which gives thee all thy might?
Spend'st thou thy fury on some worthless song,   3
Darkening thy power to lend base subjects light?   4
Return, forgetful muse, and straight redeem
In gentle numbers time so idly spent;   6
Sing to the ear that doth thy lays esteem   7
And gives thy pen both skill and argument.   8
Rise, resty muse, my love's sweet face survey,   9
If time have any wrinkle graven there;   10
If any, be a satire to decay   11
And make time's spoils despisèd everywhere.
    Give my love fame faster than time wastes life;
    So thou prevent'st his scythe and crooked knife.   14

---

3 *fury* poetic passion, *furor poeticus* 4 *Darkening* diminishing 6 *gentle numbers* noble verses 7 *lays* poems 8 *argument* subject matter 9 *resty* lazy 10 *If* to see if 11 *satire to* satirist against 14 *So . . . prevent'st* thus you forestall; *crooked knife* sickle (or perhaps simply a synonym for *scythe*, for emphasis); *crooked* (has the overtone of "malicious")

101

O truant muse, what shall be thy amends
2 For thy neglect of truth in beauty dyed?
3 Both truth and beauty on my love depends;
4 So dost thou too, and therein dignified.
5 Make answer, muse: wilt thou not haply say,
6 "Truth needs no color with his color fixed,
7 Beauty no pencil, beauty's truth to lay;
8 But best is best if never intermixed"?
Because he needs no praise, wilt thou be dumb?
10 Excuse not silence so, for't lies in thee
To make him much outlive a gilded tomb
12 And to be praised of ages yet to be.
13   Then do thy office, muse; I teach thee how,
14   To make him seem long hence as he shows now.

---

2 *in . . . dyed* thoroughly imbued with beauty 3 *love* beloved; *depends* depend 4 *therein dignified* you, my muse, are thereby dignified 5 *haply* perhaps 6 *color* (1) painting, (2) rhetoric; *color fixed* permanent, natural color ("Truth needs no color" was proverbial) 7 *pencil* brush; *lay* apply 8 *if . . . intermixed* only if never adulterated 12 *of* by 13 *office* duty 14 *shows* appears

102

My love is strengthened, though more weak in seeming;   1
I love not less, though less the show appear: 2
That love is merchandised whose rich esteeming   3
The owner's tongue doth publish everywhere.   4
Our love was new, and then but in the spring,   5
When I was wont to greet it with my lays,   6
As Philomel in summer's front doth sing   7
And stops her pipe in growth of riper days;   8
Not that the summer is less pleasant now
Than when her mournful hymns did hush the night,   10
But that wild music burdens every bough,   11
And sweets grown common lose their dear delight.   12
    Therefore, like her, I sometime hold my tongue,
    Because I would not dull you with my song.   14

---

1 *more . . . seeming* it appears weaker (because of the silence described in Sonnets 100 and 101)   2 *less . . . appear* (1) the show of love seems smaller, (2) the display is less visible   3 *merchandised* commodified, for sale; *rich esteeming* great value   4 *publish* publicize, announce   5 *in . . . spring* in its first flush   6 *lays* songs   7 *Philomel . . . front* the nightingale at the beginning of summer   8 *pipe* music; *in . . . days* as the season progresses   11 *wild music* (1) song of wild birds, (2) disordered, uncivil music   12 *dear* (1) valuable, precious, (2) loving, beloved   14 *dull you* (1) cloy you, (2) "take off your edge," "dim your brightness"

103

1 Alack, what poverty my muse brings forth,
2 That, having such a scope to show her pride,
3 The argument all bare is of more worth
  Than when it hath my added praise beside.
  O, blame me not if I no more can write!
  Look in your glass, and there appears a face
7 That overgoes my blunt invention quite,
8 Dulling my lines and doing me disgrace.
9 Were it not sinful then, striving to mend,
10 To mar the subject that before was well?
11 For to no other pass my verses tend
  Than of your graces and your gifts to tell;
13   And more, much more, than in my verse can sit
  Your own glass shows you when you look in it.

---

1 *poverty* poor stuff 2 *That . . . scope* in that, having such a great opportunity; *pride* splendor 3 *argument . . . bare* subject in itself, the naked theme 7 *overgoes* outdoes; *blunt* (1) dull, (2) crude 8 *lines* verses; *doing . . . disgrace* putting me to shame 9 *mend* improve 11 *pass* purpose; *tend* (1) are directed, (2) serve 13 *sit* reside

104

To me, fair friend, you never can be old,
For as you were when first your eye I eyed,   2
Such seems your beauty still. Three winters cold
Have from the forests shook three summers' pride,   4
Three beauteous springs to yellow autumn turned
In process of the seasons have I seen,   6
Three April perfumes in three hot Junes burned,
Since first I saw you fresh, which yet are green.   8
Ah, yet doth beauty, like a dial hand,   9
Steal from his figure, and no pace perceived;   10
So your sweet hue, which methinks still doth stand,   11
Hath motion, and mine eye may be deceived;
    For fear of which, hear this, thou age unbred: 13
    Ere you were born was beauty's summer dead.   14

---

2 *eyed* saw   4 *pride* splendor   6 *process* the progress   8 *fresh* (1) youthful, (2)
freshly, for the first time; *which* who; *green* young   9 *dial* clock   10 *Steal . . .*
figure (1) move imperceptibly from its number, (2) imperceptibly depart
from the form it inhabits   11 *sweet hue* lovely appearance; *methinks . . .*
stand (1) seems to me to remain motionless, (2) seems to me as yet un-
changed   13 *unbred* unborn   14 *beauty's summer* i.e., beauty at its best

105

Let not my love be called idolatry,
2 Nor my belovèd as an idol show,
Since all alike my songs and praises be
4 To one, of one, still such, and ever so.
Kind is my love today, tomorrow kind,
6 Still constant in a wondrous excellence;
7 Therefore my verse, to constancy confined,
8 One thing expressing, leaves out difference.
9 "Fair, kind, and true" is all my argument,
10 "Fair, kind, and true," varying to other words;
11 And in this change is my invention spent,
Three themes in one, which wondrous scope affords.
13 Fair, kind, and true have often lived alone,
14 Which three till now never kept seat in one.

---

2 *show* appear   4 *To one* (to the one god, the beloved, not the many gods of idolatry); *still . . . so* always and ever the same   6 *Still constant* (1) always faithful, (2) always the same   7 *to . . . confined* (1) limited to the subject of constancy, (2) bound to be always the same   8 *leaves . . . difference* (1) omits variety, ignores other subjects, has a single theme, (2) omits disagreements (between us)   9 *argument* subject matter   10 *varying . . . words* sometimes using other words   11 *change* variation; *invention* poetic ingenuity; *spent* (1) employed, (2) exhausted   13 *lived alone* i.e., lived separately, inhabited different individuals   14 *kept seat* made their home (a *seat* is a landowner's estate or official dwelling)

106

When in the chronicle of wasted time   1
I see descriptions of the fairest wights,   2
And beauty making beautiful old rhyme
In praise of ladies dead and lovely knights;
Then, in the blazon of sweet beauty's best,   5
Of hand, of foot, of lip, of eye, of brow,
I see their antique pen would have expressed
Even such a beauty as you master now.   8
So all their praises are but prophecies
Of this our time, all you prefiguring;   10
And, for they looked but with divining eyes,   11
They had not still enough your worth to sing: 12
    For we, which now behold these present days,
    Have eyes to wonder, but lack tongues to praise.

---

1 *wasted* (1) past, (2) ruined   2 *wights* people (of either sex; the word is archaic, and specifically, for Shakespeare's era, Spenserian)   5 *blazon* laudatory formal description (in poetics, a catalogue of praiseworthy body parts, as in l. 6; in heraldry, a coat of arms emblematically embodying the bearer's virtues) 8 *master* (1) possess, (2) control   11 *for* because; *but* merely; *divining* forecasting   12 *still* (most editors emend to "skill"; but the point is that the ancient poets *had* the requisite skill – what they lacked was the young man's actual beauty as a subject)

107

1 Not mine own fears nor the prophetic soul
  Of the wide world dreaming on things to come
3 Can yet the lease of my true love control,
4 Supposed as forfeit to a confined doom.
5 The mortal moon hath her eclipse endured,
6 And the sad augurs mock their own presage;
7 Incertainties now crown themselves assured,
8 And peace proclaims olives of endless age.
9 Now with the drops of this most balmy time
10 My love looks fresh, and Death to me subscribes,
   Since, spite of him, I'll live in this poor rhyme,
12 While he insults o'er dull and speechless tribes:
   And thou in this shalt find thy monument
14 When tyrants' crests and tombs of brass are spent.

1-2 *soul . . . world* i.e., the collective spirit of all humankind 3 *Can . . . control* i.e., fears and premonitions do not set limits to my love; *yet* (1) even so, (2) now; *lease* term (the period my love will last) 4 *Supposed . . . doom* i.e., presumed to be subject to a limited tenure; *confined doom* stipulated end 5 *The . . . endured* (a much debated line, most plausibly explained as alluding to the death in 1603 of Queen Elizabeth, regularly allegorized as the moon goddess Cynthia, but nevertheless mortal, and hence the *eclipse* is permanent); *endured* (1) suffered, (2) outlasted (the latter suggesting a different historical allegory, Elizabeth's survival of her grand climacteric, her sixty-third year, an astrologically perilous age) 6 *sad augurs* solemn prophets; *presage* predictions 7 *Incertainties . . . assured* uncertainty has now triumphed as certainty; *Incertainties* (1) unlikely things, (2) our insecurities about them 8 *olives . . . age* eternal olive branches (emblems of peace – see Genesis 8:11; if the allusion in l. 5 is indeed to the death of Elizabeth, the proclamation of peace alludes to the programmatic pacifism of her successor, James I) 9 *balmy time* endless age of peace, conceived as medicinal or healing 10 *love* (the passion, not the beloved); *to me subscribes* (1) surrenders to me, (2) validates (literally, underwrites) me 12 *insults o'er* victoriously derides; *dull . . . tribes* i.e., the multitudes who have no poetry to immortalize them 14 *crests* (1) helmets, (2) coats of arms (which adorned *tombs*); *spent* wasted away

108

What's in the brain that ink may character   1
Which hath not figured to thee my true spirit?   2
What's new to speak, what now to register,   3
That may express my love or thy dear merit?
Nothing, sweet boy; but yet, like prayers divine,
I must each day say o'er the very same;
Counting no old thing old, thou mine, I thine,   7
Even as when first I hallowed thy fair name.   8
So that eternal love in love's fresh case   9
Weighs not the dust and injury of age,   10
Nor gives to necessary wrinkles place,   11
But makes antiquity for aye his page,   12
   Finding the first conceit of love there bred   13
   Where time and outward form would show it dead.   14

---

1 *character* write 2 *figured* depicted, described; *my ... spirit* (1) the truth of my spirit, (2) my faithful spirit 3 *register* record 7 *Counting ... thing old* i.e., considering no often-repeated thing to be outmoded; *thou ... thine* you are mine, I am yours (the "old things" that remain fresh) 8 *hallowed* sanctified 9 *love's ... case* (1) love's eternally fresh circumstances, (2) love's always fresh appearance 10 *Weighs not* is not concerned with 11 *gives ... place* makes room for inevitable wrinkles 12 *makes ... page* (1) makes old age his servant forever, (2) transforms old age permanently into his page boy, (3) forever makes old things the subject of his writings 13 *first conceit* (1) original poetic idea, (2) first inkling 14 *Where* whereas; *outward form* i.e., the timeworn outward appearance

109

O, never say that I was false of heart,
2 Though absence seemed my flame to qualify;
3 As easy might I from my self depart
   As from my soul, which in thy breast doth lie.
5 That is my home of love: if I have ranged,
   Like him that travels I return again,
7 Just to the time, not with the time exchanged,
8 So that myself bring water for my stain.
   Never believe, though in my nature reigned
10 All frailties that besiege all kinds of blood,
11 That it could so preposterously be stained
12 To leave for nothing all thy sum of good;
    For nothing this wide universe I call
    Save thou, my rose; in it thou art my all.

---

2 *qualify* (1) abate, (2) call into question 3 *easy* (1) easily, (2) comfortably; *my self* i.e., my true, essential self 5 *ranged* wandered 7 *Just* punctual; *with . . . exchanged* (1) altered by my time away, (2) changed like the time 8 *bring . . . stain* expunge my own offense 10 *all kinds . . . blood* every disposition, all humanity 11 *it* (*my nature,* l. 9); *preposterously* unnaturally, perversely 12 *for nothing* (1) in favor of something worthless, (2) for no reason

110

Alas, 'tis true, I have gone here and there
And made myself a motley to the view,   2
Gored mine own thoughts, sold cheap what is most dear,   3
Made old offenses of affections new.   4
Most true it is that I have looked on truth   5
Askance and strangely; but, by all above,   6
These blenches gave my heart another youth,   7
And worse essays proved thee my best of love.   8
Now all is done, have what shall have no end: 9
Mine appetite I never more will grind   10
On newer proof, to try an older friend,   11
A god in love, to whom I am confined.   12
    Then give me welcome, next my heaven the best,   13
    Even to thy pure and most most loving breast.

---

2 *motley* fool, jester; *to . . . view* publicly, in everyone's eyes   3 *Gored* (1) wounded, (2) slashed (as cloth is, to reveal the differently colored layer underneath), (3) wearing gores (rectangular pieces of cloth used in making the fool's motley); *dear* (1) valuable, (2) loved   4 *Made . . . new* i.e., repeated the old offense of infidelity with new love affairs   5 *truth* constancy, fidelity   6 *Askance* (1) obliquely, not directly, (2) disdainfully; *strangely* as a stranger to it   7 *blenches* swervings, deviations; *gave . . . youth* made me feel young again   8 *essays* experiments (with other loves)   9 *Now . . . end* now that I'm done with all that, take what will last forever   10–11 *grind . . . proof* try out on a newer whetstone (i.e., try to sharpen my love on someone new)   11 *try* test   12 *confined* utterly faithful, devoted   13 *next . . . best* the next best thing to heaven for me

111

1 O, for my sake do you with Fortune chide,
2 The guilty goddess of my harmful deeds,
That did not better for my life provide
4 Than public means which public manners breeds.
5 Thence comes it that my name receives a brand;
6 And almost thence my nature is subdued
To what it works in, like the dyer's hand:
8 Pity me then, and wish I were renewed,
Whilst, like a willing patient, I will drink
10 Potions of eisel 'gainst my strong infection;
11 No bitterness that I will bitter think,
12 Nor double penance, to correct correction.
        Pity me then, dear friend, and I assure ye
14   Even that your pity is enough to cure me.

---

1 *O . . . chide* rebuke fortune on my behalf (*do you* is imperative) 2 *guilty . . . of* goddess responsible for 4 *public means* a livelihood dependent on the public (as an actor and playwright); *means* (1) methods, (2) resources; *public manners* (1) open, outgoing (and therefore vulgar) manners, (2) promiscuous behavior 5 *name* reputation; *brand* stigma (as criminals were branded) 6–7 *subdued / To* (1) reduced to, (2) overpowered by 8 *renewed* restored, healed 10 *eisel* vinegar (used as a medicine against the plague) 11 *No bitterness* there is no bitterness 12 *Nor . . . correction* nor will I think a double penance bitter, to correct what has been corrected (but still needs mending) 14 *Even . . . pity* that your pity alone

112

Your love and pity doth th' impression fill   1
Which vulgar scandal stamped upon my brow;   2
For what care I who calls me well or ill,
So you o'ergreen my bad, my good allow?   4
You are my all the world, and I must strive
To know my shames and praises from your tongue;
None else to me, nor I to none alive,   7
That my steeled sense or changes right or wrong.
In so profound abyss I throw all care   9
Of others' voices that my adder's sense   10
To critic and to flatterer stoppèd are;
Mark how with my neglect I do dispense: 12
   You are so strongly in my purpose bred   13
   That all the world besides methinks they're dead.   14

---

1 *th' impression fill* erase the scar (of the *brand* in Sonnet 111, l. 5)   2 *vulgar scandal* (anything from malicious gossip to public disgrace, or possibly simply the scandal of being *public*, as in Sonnet 111, l. 4)   4 *o'ergreen* cover over, reseed   7–8 *None . . . wrong* i.e., there is no one else who exists for me, or for whom I exist, who makes my hardened nature (*steeled sense*) change for either good or ill   9 *profound* deep   10 *Of* about; *adder's sense* deaf ears (adders were proverbially deaf)   12 *Mark . . . dispense* note how I excuse my disregard (of *vulgar scandal*, l. 2)   13 *strongly . . . bred* powerfully imbued in my intentions   14 *all . . . besides* the rest of the world other than you

113

1 Since I left you, mine eye is in my mind,
2 And that which governs me to go about
3 Doth part his function and is partly blind,
4 Seems seeing, but effectually is out;
   For it no form delivers to the heart
6 Of bird, of flower, or shape which it doth latch;
7 Of his quick objects hath the mind no part,
8 Nor his own vision holds what it doth catch;
9 For if it see the rud'st or gentlest sight,
10 The most sweet favor or deformèd'st creature,
   The mountain or the sea, the day or night,
12 The crow or dove, it shapes them to your feature.
      Incapable of more, replete with you,
      My most true mind thus maketh mine eye untrue.

---

1 *mine . . . mind* I see with my mind's eye 2 *governs . . . about* directs my steps 3 *Doth part* (1) divides, (2) departs from, (3) does only part of 4 *Seems seeing* seems to see; *effectually* in effect; *out* (1) extinguished (like a light), (2) off, not performing its function 6 *latch* catch sight of 7 *his* its (the eye's); *quick* (1) fleeting, (2) living 8 *Nor . . . holds* nor does the eye itself retain 9 *rud'st or gentlest* (1) most base or most noble, (2) most crude or most cultured, (3) most savage or most civilized, (4) most coarse or most delicate, etc. 10 *favor* face 12 *feature* form, likeness

114

Or whether doth my mind, being crowned with you,   1
Drink up the monarch's plague, this flattery?   2
Or whether shall I say mine eye saith true,
And that your love taught it this alchemy,   4
To make of monsters and things indigest   5
Such cherubins as your sweet self resemble,   6
Creating every bad a perfect best
As fast as objects to his beams assemble?   8
O, 'tis the first; 'tis flattery in my seeing,
And my great mind most kingly drinks it up: 10
Mine eye well knows what with his gust is 'greeing   11
And to his palate doth prepare the cup.   12
   If it be poisoned, 'tis the lesser sin
   That mine eye loves it and doth first begin.   14

1, 3 *Or whether . . . Or whether* i.e., is this the case, or is that? 1 *being . . . with* made a king by loving you 2 *this flattery* i.e., does my eye merely flatter my mind? 4 *your love* loving you 5 *indigest* shapeless 6 *cherubins* angels; *as . . . resemble* as resemble you (not "as you resemble") 8 *As . . . assemble* as quickly as objects gather in his sight (the eye was thought to see by emitting beams of light) 11 *what . . . 'greeing* what pleases its taste 12 *to . . . palate* to suit my mind's taste 14 *That . . . begin* i.e., since my eye takes the first drink

115

Those lines that I before have writ do lie,
2 Even those that said I could not love you dearer;
Yet then my judgment knew no reason why
4 My most full flame should afterwards burn clearer.
5 But reckoning time, whose millioned accidents
Creep in 'twixt vows and change decrees of kings,
7 Tan sacred beauty, blunt the sharp'st intents,
8 Divert strong minds to th' course of alt'ring things –
Alas, why, fearing of time's tyranny,
10 Might I not then say, "Now I love you best"
11 When I was certain o'er incertainty,
12 Crowning the present, doubting of the rest?
13   Love is a babe; then might I not say so,
    To give full growth to that which still doth grow.

2 *Even* namely 4 *most full* (1) as intense as possible, (2) very intense (the meaning changes from 1 to 2 as the poem progresses); *clearer* more brightly 5 *reckoning time* (1) taking time into account, (2) as Time (personified) keeps count; *millioned accidents* millions of misfortunes 7 *Tan* darken, coarsen 8 *Divert . . . things* deflect strong minds into accepting the flow of mutability, carry them along with the current of change 10 *Might . . . say* could I not then have said 11 *certain . . . incertainty* absolutely certain 12 *Crowning . . . rest* making the present king, denying the reality of anything else 13 *then* therefore; *say so* say *Now I love you best*

116

Let me not to the marriage of true minds   1
Admit impediments; love is not love   2
Which alters when it alteration finds   3
Or bends with the remover to remove.   4
O, no, it is an ever-fixèd mark   5
That looks on tempests and is never shaken;
It is the star to every wand'ring bark,   7
Whose worth's unknown, although his height be taken.   8
Love's not time's fool, though rosy lips and cheeks   9
Within his bending sickle's compass come;   10
Love alters not with his brief hours and weeks,   11
But bears it out even to the edge of doom.   12
   If this be error, and upon me proved,   13
   I never writ, nor no man ever loved.   14

---

1 *Let me not* i.e., I would never 2 *Admit impediments* concede that there are obstacles (echoing the *marriage* service, which calls on anyone who knows of "any impediment" to the marriage to declare it) 3 *Which . . . finds* (the *impediments* that are denied now clearly come from within the *marriage*, not from without); *alteration* (1) changes of heart, (2) changes effected by time or circumstance 4 *bends . . . remove* inclines to separate because the lover does 5 *mark* lighthouse 7 *star* polestar; *bark* boat 8 *worth's unknown* value is incalculable; *his . . . taken* its altitude can be calculated 9 *Love's . . . fool* time cannot make a fool of love (i.e., love is not subject to time) 10 *bending* (1) curved, (2) causing (what it mows) to bend; *compass* range 11 *his* (1) love's, (2) time's 12 *bears . . . doom* endures even to doomsday 13 *error* (1) legally, a fault in procedure invalidating the judgment, (2) theologically, heresy 14 *no . . . loved* (1) no man has ever been in love, (2) I never loved any man (i.e., the man who is the subject of these sonnets)

117

1 Accuse me thus, that I have scanted all
2 Wherein I should your great deserts repay;
3 Forgot upon your dearest love to call,
4 Whereto all bonds do tie me day by day;
5 That I have frequent been with unknown minds
6 And given to time your own dear-purchased right;
That I have hoisted sail to all the winds
Which should transport me farthest from your sight.
9 Book both my willfulness and errors down,
10 And on just proof surmise accumulate;
11 Bring me within the level of your frown,
12 But shoot not at me in your wakened hate:
13 Since my appeal says I did strive to prove
14 The constancy and virtue of your love.

---

1 *Accuse . . . thus* (the poet draws up the case against himself); *scanted* slighted, neglected 2 *deserts* virtues (specifically, what you deserve from me) 3 *call* invoke (with a suggestion of prayer) 4 *bonds* (1) obligations, (2) oaths (as in the *marriage of true minds*, Sonnet 116) 5 *frequent* familiar; *unknown minds* i.e, people I don't even know 6 *given . . . right* i.e., wasted the time that was by all rights yours; *dear-purchased* dearly bought 9 *Book . . . down* record both my deliberate and my unintentional trespasses; *errors* (literally, "wanderings") 10 *on . . . accumulate* add to what you can absolutely prove whatever you suspect 11 *level* aim, range 12 *wakened* newly aroused 13 *appeal* (1) plea in my defense, (2) appeal against an inevitably unfavorable judgment; *prove* test 14 *virtue* (1) strength, (2) moral superiority

118

Like as to make our appetites more keen,   1
With eager compounds we our palate urge;   2
As to prevent our maladies unseen,   3
We sicken to shun sickness when we purge: 4
Even so, being full of your ne'er-cloying sweetness,   5
To bitter sauces did I frame my feeding;   6
And, sick of welfare, found a kind of meetness   7
To be diseased ere that there was true needing.   8
Thus policy in love, t' anticipate   9
The ills that were not, grew to faults assured,   10
And brought to medicine a healthful state   11
Which, rank of goodness, would by ill be cured.   12
   But thence I learn, and find the lesson true,
   Drugs poison him that so fell sick of you.   14

---

1 *Like as* just as   2 *eager compounds* spicy sauces, sharp condiments; *urge* stimulate   3 *prevent* forestall; *unseen* (1) not yet present, (2) with no symptoms   4 *sicken ... purge* (Renaissance laxatives were powerful and notoriously unpalatable)   5 *Even so* in the same way   6 *To ... sauces* i.e., around unsavory company; *frame* organize   7 *sick of welfare* (1) surfeited with good food, (2) sick of good health; *meetness* appropriateness   8 *ere ... needing* before there was any real need to be   9 *policy* strategy, politics; *anticipate* forestall, prevent   10 *ills* (1) illnesses, (2) evils; *grew ... assured* (1) turned to actual diseases, (2) turned to real misbehavior   11 *brought ... medicine* i.e., required medical treatment for   12 *rank of* (1) too full of, (2) made sick by; *would* wants to   14 *so* thus

119

1 What potions have I drunk of siren tears
2 Distilled from limbecks foul as hell within,
3 Applying fears to hopes and hopes to fears,
4 Still losing when I saw myself to win!
  What wretched errors hath my heart committed,
6 Whilst it hath thought itself so blessèd never!
7 How have mine eyes out of their spheres been fitted
  In the distraction of this madding fever!
  O, benefit of ill! Now I find true
10 That better is by evil still made better;
  And ruined love, when it is built anew,
  Grows fairer than at first, more strong, far greater.
    So I return rebuked to my content,
    And gain by ills thrice more than I have spent.

---

1 *potions* drugged drinks; *siren tears* i.e., dangerous temptations (the sirens were sea creatures whose beautiful, seductive songs lured sailors to their death; Odysseus survived the experience by having his sailors seal their ears with wax and tie him to the mast, so he could hear them without danger) 2 *limbecks . . . within* diabolical internal alembics, the sirens as alchemical retorts 3 *Applying . . . to fears* using fears as medicine for hopes, and hopes for fears 4 *Still* always; *saw myself* expected 6 *so . . . never* never happier 7 *out . . . fitted* started out of their sockets (or, analogized to stars, out of their *spheres*) 10 *better . . . better* good things are always made better by experiencing evil

120

That you were once unkind befriends me now,
And for that sorrow which I then did feel   2
Needs must I under my transgression bow,   3
Unless my nerves were brass or hammered steel.   4
For if you were by my unkindness shaken,
As I by yours, you've passed a hell of time,
And I, a tyrant, have no leisure taken   7
To weigh how once I suffered in your crime.
O that our night of woe might have remembered   9
My deepest sense how hard true sorrow hits,   10
And soon to you, as you to me then, tendered
The humble salve which wounded bosoms fits!   12
    But that your trespass now becomes a fee;   13
    Mine ransoms yours, and yours must ransom me.   14

---

2 *for* because of   3 *my transgression* my unkindness to you (as in Sonnet 119)
4 *nerves* (1) sinews, (2) feelings   7–8 *have . . . weigh* have not paused to con-
sider   9 *night of woe* i.e., dark period of estrangement; *remembered* reminded
12 *salve* i.e., apology as a soothing balm; *fits* suits   13 *that . . . trespass* that
transgression of yours; *fee* payment   14 *ransoms* repays, redeems

121

1 'Tis better to be vile than vile esteemed
2 When not to be receives reproach of being,
3 And the just pleasure lost, which is so deemed
   Not by our feeling but by others' seeing.
5 For why should others' false adulterate eyes
6 Give salutation to my sportive blood?
7 Or on my frailties why are frailer spies,
8 Which in their wills count bad what I think good?
9 No, I am that I am; and they that level
10 At my abuses reckon up their own:
11 I may be straight though they themselves be bevel;
12 By their rank thoughts my deeds must not be shown,
13   Unless this general evil they maintain:
14   All men are bad and in their badness reign.

---

1 *vile esteemed* thought to be vile   2 *to be* i.e., to be *vile*; *being* being *vile*
3 *the ... lost* (1) you don't even have the fun of being wicked, (2) the plea-
sure you are legitimately entitled to (in not being wicked) is lost   3–4
which ... seeing i.e., the pleasure is *lost* not because of how we feel, but be-
cause of how others regard it   3 *so deemed* considered *vile*   5 *adulterate* cor-
rupt   6 *Give ... to* greet, hail as a friend; *sportive blood* (1) high spirits, (2)
sexual energy   7 *on ... spies* why do those with more faults than mine spy
out my faults   8 *in ... wills* willfully   9 *I ... am* i.e., and nobody's bad
opinion will change me (ironically quoting God's words to Moses from the
burning bush, Exodus 3:14)   9–10 *level / At* (1) guess at, (2) take aim at
(i.e., criticize)   10 *abuses* faults; *reckon up* merely sum up   11 *straight* hon-
est; *bevel* crooked, dishonest   12 *By* through; *rank* (1) lustful, (2) corrupt
13 *general evil* (1) precept about evil, (2) universal evil; *maintain* demon-
strate   14 *in ... reign* through their wickedness prosper

122

Thy gift, thy tables, are within my brain   1
Full charactered with lasting memory,   2
Which shall above that idle rank remain   3
Beyond all date, even to eternity;   4
Or, at the least, so long as brain and heart
Have faculty by nature to subsist,   6
Till each to razed oblivion yield his part   7
Of thee, thy record never can be missed.   8
That poor retention could not so much hold,   9
Nor need I tallies thy dear love to score;   10
Therefore to give them from me was I bold,   11
To trust those tables that receive thee more.   12
  To keep an adjunct to remember thee   13
  Were to import forgetfulness in me.   14

---

1 *tables* notebook (presumably blank, for the poet to write in; see Sonnet 77)
2 *Full charactered* fully inscribed   3 *Which . . . remain* i.e., lasting memory
will endure longer than the trifling verses written in the notebook; *idle rank*
(1) useless status, (2) trivial lines of verse   4 *date* limit of time   6 *faculty . . .
subsist* natural power to survive   7 *razed oblivion* oblivion that destroys
everything; *his* its   8 *missed* lost   9 *retention* container (i.e., the notebook)
10 *tallies* reckonings   11 *to . . . me* to give the notebook away   12 *those ta-
bles* "the table of my memory" (*Hamlet*, I.5.98)   13 *adjunct* artificial aid   14
import imply

123

No, Time, thou shalt not boast that I do change:
2 Thy pyramids built up with newer might
To me are nothing novel, nothing strange;
4 They are but dressings of a former sight.
5 Our dates are brief, and therefore we admire
What thou dost foist upon us that is old,
7 And rather make them born to our desire
8 Than think that we before have heard them told.
9 Thy registers and thee I both defy,
10 Not wondering at the present nor the past;
11 For thy records and what we see doth lie,
12 Made more or less by thy continual haste.
This I do vow, and this shall ever be:
I will be true, despite thy scythe and thee.

---

2 *pyramids* i.e., monuments or monumental buildings; *newer might* modern skill 4 *dressings* dressing up, refurbishing; *a former sight* things we've seen before 5 *dates* life spans 7 *rather . . . desire* prefer to believe them newly created according to our taste 8 *think* (1) believe, (2) remember 9 *registers* records 11 *thy . . . see* i.e., both chronicles and our own experience; *records* (accented on the second syllable) 12 *Made . . . haste* i.e., time's onward rush makes us misjudge things; *more or less* greater or lesser than they really are

124

If my dear love were but the child of state,	1
It might for Fortune's bastard be unfathered,	2
As subject to Time's love or to Time's hate,	3
Weeds among weeds, or flowers with flowers gathered.	4
No, it was builded far from accident;	5
It suffers not in smiling pomp, nor falls	6
Under the blow of thrallèd discontent,	7
Whereto th' inviting time our fashion calls:	8
It fears not policy, that heretic	9
Which works on leases of short-numbered hours,	10
But all alone stands hugely politic,	11
That it nor grows with heat nor drowns with showers.	12
To this I witness call the fools of Time,	13
Which die for goodness, who have lived for crime.	14

1 *my . . . love* my love for you; *but . . . state* merely dependent on circumstance (e.g., prompted by your wealth and position)   2 *for . . . unfathered* as the child of Fortune have no legitimate father (but since the love is real, and heartfelt, the young man is its father)   3 *to Time's . . . hate* i.e., to the capriciousness of Fortune   4 *Weeds . . . gathered* i.e., as commonplace as these   5 *far . . . accident* i.e., had nothing to do with chance   6 *suffers . . . in* is unaffected by; *smiling pomp* the smiles of the great   7 *thrallèd discontent* (1) enslavement to (my own) discontent, (2) those who are slaves to their unhappiness   8 *Whereto . . . calls* to which the present time tempts people like me (*our fashion*)   9 *policy . . . heretic* expediency, that false doctrine   10 *works on leases . . . hours* i.e., takes short views (unlike love, whose lease is eternal)   11 *But . . . politic* i.e., only love is extremely practical   12 *That it nor* since it neither   13 *fools . . . Time* dupes of time, timeservers, opportunists   14 *Which . . . goodness* i.e., who repent at the last moment

125

1 Were't aught to me I bore the canopy,
2 With my extern the outward honoring,
3 Or laid great bases for eternity,
4 Which proves more short than waste or ruining?
5 Have I not seen dwellers on form and favor
6 Lose all and more by paying too much rent,
7 For compound sweet forgoing simple savor,
8 Pitiful thrivers, in their gazing spent?
9 No, let me be obsequious in thy heart,
10 And take thou my oblation, poor but free,
11 Which is not mixed with seconds, knows no art
12 But mutual render, only me for thee.
13 　　Hence, thou suborned informer; a true soul
14 　　When most impeached stands least in thy control.

---

1 *Were't . . . me* would it matter to me; *I . . . canopy* (the canopy was ceremonially carried above the central figure in aristocratic processions – hence "I was honored by attending on the great") 2 *With . . . honoring* with my appearance paying homage to the appearance (of the great) 3 *great bases* huge foundations; *for eternity* designed to last forever 4 *proves* prove; *waste . . . ruining* destruction or decay 5 *dwellers on* i.e., those who dwell on or overvalue (punning on "tenants"); *form . . . favor* (1) decorum and honor, (2) shape and appearance, (3) body and face 6 *by . . . rent* i.e., through their extravagant concern for externals 7 *compound sweet* complex pleasures 8 *Pitiful thrivers* pathetic successes; *in . . . spent* bankrupted by their fascination 9 *in . . . heart* (instead of at court) 10 *oblation* offering; *free* freely given 11 *seconds* second-best, inferior matter; *art* artifice 12 *mutual render* fully equal interchange 13 *suborned informer* bribed or intimidated (and therefore false) witness; *a . . . soul* i.e., such as myself 14 *impeached* accused; *stands . . . control* is least in your power (i.e., the power of the false witness against true love)

Turn to Dark Lady

126

O thou, my lovely boy, who in thy power 1
Dost hold Time's fickle glass, his sickle hour; 2
Who hast by waning grown, and therein show'st 3
Thy lovers withering as thy sweet self grow'st; 4
If Nature, sovereign mistress over wrack, 5
As thou goest onwards, still will pluck thee back, 6
She keeps thee to this purpose, that her skill 7
May Time disgrace and wretched minutes kill. 8
Yet fear her, O thou minion of her pleasure! 9
She may detain, but not still keep, her treasure; 10
Her audit, though delayed, answered must be, 11
And her quietus is to render thee. 12
[   ] 13
[   ]

Rhyme scheme = all couplets

Given its place in the sequence, the poem bids farewell to the beloved young man. Its form, twelve lines of couplets rather than the traditional sonnet, also interrupts the sequence stylistically.
1 *lovely boy* i.e., the young man (not Cupid, who would not in the final lines be subject to time and death) 2 *glass* hourglass (*fickle* because constantly running); *his sickle hour* the time when Time's sickle strikes 3 *hast . . . grown* has grown more lovely by aging; *therein show'st* thereby shows in contrast 5 *wrack* ruin 6 *thou goest onwards* i.e., you grow older 7 *to* for 8 *wretched . . . kill* i.e., demolish even the smallest units of time (seconds were not used till the mid-seventeenth century) 9 *minion* (1) darling, (2) servant 11 *audit* final reckoning 12 *quietus* quittance, release from obligation; *render* surrender 13–14 (Q makes up the sonnet's fourteen lines typographically by appending two sets of empty parentheses, represented here as brackets, as if to say that despite all the sonnets and all the couplets, there is still no conclusion to this erotic history. It is not inconceivable that the parentheses are authorial, but they are more likely to be the work of the original editor, who clearly felt that something was missing.)

127

1 In the old age black was not counted fair,
2 Or, if it were, it bore not beauty's name;
3 But now is black beauty's successive heir,
4 And beauty slandered with a bastard shame;
5 For since each hand hath put on nature's power,
6 Fairing the foul with art's false borrowed face,
7 Sweet beauty hath no name, no holy bower,
8 But is profaned, if not lives in disgrace.
   Therefore my mistress' eyes are raven black,
10 Her brows so suited, and they mourners seem
11 At such who, not born fair, no beauty lack,
12 Sland'ring creation with a false esteem:
13   Yet so they mourn, becoming of their woe,
       That every tongue says beauty should look so.

In Sonnets 127–152, the poet's erotic attention turns from the fair youth to a dark mistress. Reading the sonnets as a narrative, it is reasonable to identify her with the disruptive woman of Sonnets 40–42, with whom the young man betrays the poet's love. Much critical attention has been devoted to finding a real dark lady behind Shakespeare's imaginative creation, but the number of possible candidates is as large as the number of brunettes in Elizabethan London. Moreover, just as the rival poet may be a composite or a function of the developing theme of poetry and love, so also the rival beloved – the anti-Petrarchan mistress, the antithesis of the idealized male lover – may be; and it has often been observed that Shakespeare's dark lady has a poetic precedent in the black eyes and hair of Sidney's Stella.

1 *old age* past; *black* dark coloring (including dark hair and a dark complexion); *counted fair* (1) considered beautiful, (2) called blond 2 *if . . . name* i.e., even if it was considered attractive, it was not the standard of beauty 3 *successive* legitimate 4 *a . . . shame* the disgrace of bastardy 5 *put on* usurped (punning on the putting on of makeup) 6 *Fairing* beautifying 7 *no name* (1) no reputation, (2) no family name (because illegitimate); *no . . . bower* i.e., no place where it is worshiped 8 *lives . . . disgrace* (1) dishonored, (2) disfigured 10 *brows* eyebrows; *so suited* i.e., also black 11 *At* for 12 *Sland'ring . . . esteem* dishonoring nature's work by esteeming artificial beauty 13 *becoming . . . woe* with their woe so becoming to them

128

How oft, when thou, my music, music play'st
Upon that blessèd wood whose motion sounds   2
With thy sweet fingers when thou gently sway'st   3
The wiry concord that mine ear confounds,   4
Do I envy those jacks that nimble leap   5
To kiss the tender inward of thy hand,
Whilst my poor lips, which should that harvest reap,
At the wood's boldness by thee blushing stand.   8
To be so tickled they would change their state   9
And situation with those dancing chips   10
O'er whom thy fingers walk with gentle gait,
Making dead wood more blessed than living lips.
    Since saucy jacks so happy are in this,   13
    Give them thy fingers, me thy lips to kiss.

---

2 *wood* keys of the virginal (an early keyboard instrument with plucked strings); *motion* movement; *sounds* (1) resounds, (2) causes (*The wiry concord*, l. 4) to sound   3 *thou . . . sway'st* you . . . control   4 *wiry concord* harmony of strings; *mine . . . confounds* overwhelms my hearing   5 *those jacks* what plucks the string (but here, both keys and jacks, the whole mechanism)   8 *by* beside   9–10 *state . . . situation* status and location   10 *chips* pieces of wood   13 *happy* lucky

129

1 Th' expense of spirit in a waste of shame
2 Is lust in action; and, till action, lust
3 Is perjured, murd'rous, bloody, full of blame,
4 Savage, extreme, rude, cruel, not to trust;
5 Enjoyed no sooner but despisèd straight;
6 Past reason hunted, and no sooner had,
  Past reason hated as a swallowed bait
  On purpose laid to make the taker mad:
9 Made in pursuit and in possession so;
10 Had, having, and in quest to have, extreme;
11 A bliss in proof, and proved, a very woe;
12 Before, a joy proposed; behind, a dream.
  All this the world well knows, yet none knows well
14   To shun the heaven that leads men to this hell.

---

1 *spirit* (1) semen, (2) vital energy   2 *action* the sexual act, consummation
3 *full of blame* (1) totally guilty, (2) full of recriminations   4 *rude* brutal; *not to trust* not to be trusted   5 *straight* immediately   6 *Past . . . hunted* insanely sought   9 *Made* (since Malone in 1780, Q's verb has been universally and unnecessarily emended to the adjective "mad," significantly reducing the energy of the line); *so* i.e., made *mad*   11 *in proof . . . proved* both during action and once done (Q, and all editions until Malone's in 1780, read "proud." Orthographically, this could, in 1609, though not in editions after that of 1640, be read as either "proud" or "provd" – though for the latter, considering the compositor's practice in the rest of the volume, "prou'd" would have been the expected form – but, as with "travail"/*travel* in Sonnet 27, the reader of 1609 who saw "proved" in the word would not have seen only that, and would have read it as both: "provd" retained the sense of "proud," entirely appropriately, for the poem; "Pride," says the Bible, is what

129

TH'expence of Spirit in a waſte of ſhame
Is luſt in action, and till action, luſt
Is periurd, murdrous, blouddy full of blame,
Sauage, extreame, rude, cruell, not to truſt,
Inioyd no ſooner but diſpiſed ſtraight,
Paſt reaſon hunted, and no ſooner had
Paſt reaſon hated as a ſwollowed bayt,
On purpoſe layd to make the taker mad.
Made In purſut and in poſſeſſion ſo,
Had, hauing, and in queſt, to haue extreame,
A bliſſe in proofe and proud and very wo,
Before a ioy propoſd behind a dreame,

    All this the world well knowes yet none knowes well,
    To ſhun the heauen that leads men to this hell.

Sonnet 129 as it appears in the 1609 quarto.

"goeth before . . . a fall" [Proverbs 16:18] – before *very woe,* before *this hell*
[l. 14]. "Proud" also means erect or tumescent – see Sonnet 151, l. 10; still
current today in the medical term "proud flesh." It is also worth observing
that whatever Shakespeare intended, there is no evidence that anyone before
1780 ever read the word as anything but "proud."); *a* ("and" in Q – *lust*
thereby becomes *bliss, proud, woe,* in action and after completion, all at once,
a set of simultaneous and incompatible experiences; the word "and" is uni-
versally emended to *a* since Malone because it contradicts ll. 5 and 7, but it
is entirely possible that "and" is in fact correct, and introduces a change in
the argument); *very woe* i.e., truly woe, woe indeed   12 *dream* (fleeting,
delusive, but now not *despisèd* or *hated,* and *woe* only because one awakes –
l. 12 does not simply replicate the sense of ll. 5 and 11)   14 *To shun* how to
shun

130

My mistress' eyes are nothing like the sun;
Coral is far more red than her lips' red;
If snow be white, why then her breasts are dun;
4   If hairs be wires, black wires grow on her head.
5   I have seen roses damasked, red and white,
But no such roses see I in her cheeks;
And in some perfumes is there more delight
8   Than in the breath that from my mistress reeks.
I love to hear her speak; yet well I know
10 That music hath a far more pleasing sound:
11 I grant I never saw a goddess go;
12 My mistress, when she walks, treads on the ground.
    And yet, by heaven, I think my love as rare
14   As any she belied with false compare.

The sonnet plays on conventional tropes of idealization in Petrarchan poetry.
4 *wires* (as the conventional sonnet mistress is said to have hair of spun gold)
5 *damasked* (1) mingled, (2) soft, smooth   8 *reeks* emanates (not pejorative
until the eighteenth century)   11 *go* walk   12 *treads . . . ground* i.e., as mor-
tals do   14 *she* woman; *false compare* artificial comparisons

131

Thou art as tyrannous, so as thou art,   1
As those whose beauties proudly make them cruel;
For well thou know'st to my dear doting heart   3
Thou art the fairest and most precious jewel.   4
Yet in good faith some say that thee behold   5
Thy face hath not the power to make love groan;
To say they err I dare not be so bold,
Although I swear it to myself alone.
And, to be sure that is not false I swear,   9
A thousand groans, but thinking on thy face,   10
One on another's neck do witness bear   11
Thy black is fairest in my judgment's place.   12
   In nothing art thou black save in thy deeds,   13
   And thence this slander as I think proceeds.   14

---

1 *so . . . art* just as you are (dark, not fair)   3 *dear doting* (1) fondly doting, (2) tender and doting   4 *fairest* (though dark)   5 *in . . . faith* (1) indeed, (2) in all honesty   9 *to . . . sure* i.e., as proof   10 *but . . . on* when I merely think of   11 *One . . . neck* in quick succession   12 *judgment's place* considered opinion   13 *black* foul, immoral   14 *as I think* (1) in my opinion, (2) as I consider the matter

132

1 Thine eyes I love, and they, as pitying me,
2 Knowing thy heart torment me with disdain,
3 Have put on black and loving mourners be,
4 Looking with pretty ruth upon my pain.
5 And truly not the morning sun of heaven
Better becomes the gray cheeks of the east,
7 Nor that full star that ushers in the even
8 Doth half that glory to the sober west
As those two mourning eyes become thy face.
10 O, let it then as well beseem thy heart
To mourn for me, since mourning doth thee grace,
12 And suit thy pity like in every part.
Then will I swear beauty herself is black,
14 And all they foul that thy complexion lack.

---

1 *as* as if   2 *torment* to torment (an infinitive)   3 *Have . . . black* i.e., have
black eyebrows (cf. Sonnet 127, l. 10)   4 *ruth* pity   5 *morning* (punning on
"mourning")   7 *that full star . . . even* Hesperus, the evening star; *full* bright
8 *Doth* renders   10 *as . . . beseem* equally well become your heart   12 *suit . . .
like* dress your pity in the same way; *every part* i.e., heart as well as eyes   14
complexion (1) coloring, (2) disposition

133

Beshrew that heart that makes my heart to groan   1
For that deep wound it gives my friend and me: 2
Is't not enough to torture me alone,
But slave to slavery my sweet'st friend must be?   4
Me from myself thy cruel eye hath taken,
And my next self thou harder hast engrossed;   6
Of him, myself, and thee I am forsaken,
A torment thrice threefold thus to be crossed.   8
Prison my heart in thy steel bosom's ward,   9
But then my friend's heart let my poor heart bail;   10
Whoe'er keeps me, let my heart be his guard: 11
Thou canst not then use rigor in my jail.   12
    And yet thou wilt; for I, being pent in thee,   13
    Perforce am thine, and all that is in me.   14

---

1 *Beshrew* (a mild oath – "alas for") 2 *my friend* (cf. the love triangle in Sonnets 40–42) 4 *to slavery* i.e., to the same slavery you impose on me 6 *my . . . self* my other self (the friend; see Sonnet 39); *harder* more severely; *engrossed* enslaved, monopolized 8 *crossed* afflicted 9 *ward* cell 10 *bail* release (from your bondage) 11 *keeps me* imprisons me; *be . . . guard* imprison him 12 *rigor* cruelty 13 *pent* imprisoned 14 *Perforce* necessarily; *all* so is all

134

1 So, now I have confessed that he is thine
2 And I myself am mortgaged to thy will,
3 Myself I'll forfeit, so that other mine
4 Thou wilt restore to be my comfort still:
5 But thou wilt not, nor he will not be free,
6 For thou art covetous, and he is kind;
7 He learned but surety-like to write for me
  Under that bond that him as fast doth bind.
9 The statute of thy beauty thou wilt take,
10 Thou usurer that put'st forth all to use,
11 And sue a friend came debtor for my sake;
12 So him I lose through my unkind abuse.
    Him have I lost, thou hast both him and me;
14   He pays the whole, and yet am I not free.

---

1 *now* now that   2 *mortgaged to* required to obey (and subject to forfeiture if I do not); *will* (1) desire, (2) lust, (3) purposes   3 *that . . . mine* my other self (i.e., the friend; see Sonnet 133, l. 6)   4 *restore* give back to me   5 *nor . . . be* (1) nor will he be, (2) nor does he wish to be   6 *kind* (1) compliant, (2) generous   7–8 *He . . . bind* i.e., he only agreed to underwrite the bond that binds me to you, but it now binds him just as securely (presumably the friend was sent to intercede with the lady on the poet's behalf, but fell in love with her himself)   9 *The . . . take* i.e., you will exact the forfeit provided by the contract that your beauty constitutes   10 *that . . . use* (1) who demands interest on everything, (2) who turns everything into sex   11 *came debtor* who became a debtor   12 *my . . . abuse* (1) my misuse of my friend (in making him my go-between), (2) your mistreatment of me   14 *He . . . whole* (1) he is the forfeit, he satisfies the debt, (2) he fills you sexually (with *whole* punning on "hole")

135

Whoever hath her wish, thou hast thy Will,
And Will to boot, and Will in overplus.   2
More than enough am I that vex thee still,   3
To thy sweet will making addition thus.   4
Wilt thou, whose will is large and spacious,   5
Not once vouchsafe to hide my will in thine?   6
Shall will in others seem right gracious,
And in my will no fair acceptance shine?   8
The sea, all water, yet receives rain still
And in abundance addeth to his store;   10
So thou, being rich in Will, add to thy Will
One will of mine to make thy large Will more.
 Let no unkind, no fair beseechers kill;   13
 Think all but one, and me in that one Will.   14

The sonnet plays on the name *Will* (the name not only of the poet but apparently also of the woman's husband and possibly of the friend) as well as on the various meanings of the noun, including its slang usage, for both vagina and penis. In Q, the word is capitalized and italicized in Sonnets 135, 136, and 143. (See the frontispiece.)

2 *to boot* in addition **3** *vex* (1) annoy, (2) importune, stir up sexually; *still* constantly **4** *will* sexual desire; *making . . . thus* i.e., adding my own through sexual activity, through being *More than enough* **5** *spacious* (like *gracious*, l. 7, three syllables) **5, 6** *will* (playing on the sexual meanings) **6** *vouchsafe* consent **8** *in . . . will* in the case of my will; *acceptance* reception (with a sexual innuendo) **10** *his* its **13** *no unkind* (1) no unkindness, (2) the unkind word *no* **14** *Think . . . Will* i.e., think of them all as one lover, and include me (with the final *Will* including all the possible senses)

136

1   If thy soul check thee that I come so near,
2   Swear to thy blind soul that I was thy Will,
     And will, thy soul knows, is admitted there:
4   Thus far for love my love suit, sweet, fulfill.
5   Will will fulfill the treasure of thy love
     Ay, fill it full with wills, and my will one.
7   In things of great receipt with ease we prove,
8   Among a number one is reckoned none.
9   Then in the number let me pass untold,
10   Though in thy store's account I one must be;
11   For nothing hold me, so it please thee hold
     That nothing me, a some-thing, sweet, to thee.
13   Make but my name thy love, and love that still,
         And then thou lovest me, for my name is Will.

---

1 *check* rebuke; *come so near* (1) understand you so well, (2) am so open with you, (3) am so intimate with you 2 *blind* ignorant, obtuse; *thy Will* (playing on the fact that there is more than one Will involved – see Sonnet 135) 4 *fulfill* grant 5 *fulfill* fill full; *treasure* treasury (i.e., rich place, vagina) 7 *In . . . receipt* (1) in matters of great importance, (2) in receptacles of great capacity, (3) in the case of objects of large size; *with . . . prove* (1) we easily demonstrate, (2) we perform the act without difficulty 8 *Among . . . none* i.e., one does not count as a number 9 *number* accounting (of all your Wills); *untold* uncounted 10 *thy . . . account* i.e., the inventory of your lovers 11 *For . . . me* consider me worthless 11–12 *hold . . . some-thing* (1) still hold within you the *thing* of the nothing that I am (with Q's hyphenated spelling retaining the sexual implication of *thing*, penis), (2) consider the nothing that I am still something 13, 14 *my name* i.e., (1) Will, (2) desire, (3) my penis

137

Thou blind fool, Love, what dost thou to mine eyes   1
That they behold and see not what they see?   2
They know what beauty is, see where it lies,   3
Yet what the best is take the worst to be.
If eyes, corrupt by overpartial looks,   5
Be anchored in the bay where all men ride,   6
Why of eyes' falsehood hast thou forgèd hooks,   7
Whereto the judgment of my heart is tied?
Why should my heart think that a several plot   9
Which my heart knows the wide world's common place?   10
Or mine eyes seeing this, say this is not,   11
To put fair truth upon so foul a face?
   In things right true my heart and eyes have erred,   13
   And to this false plague are they now transferred.   14

---

1 *blind* (Cupid is traditionally represented as blindfolded)   2 *see not* do not understand   3 *lies* (1) resides, (2) deceives   5 *corrupt* corrupted; *overpartial* too admiring and adoring, and thus prejudiced   6 *Be . . . ride* i.e., drop my anchor where every other man does   7 *eyes' . . . hooks* (the image now is of hooks and eyes as fasteners); *thou* (*Love* is still being addressed)   9 *think . . . plot* i.e., believe that is a private place (i.e., that you belong to me alone)   10 *knows* knows to be; *common place* place open to everyone (with a quibble on "commonplace," something everyone knows)   11 *mine eyes* why should my eyes   13 *In . . . erred* i.e., I have misjudged what is genuinely good   14 *false plague* (1) disease of falsehood, (2) infectious, faithless woman; *transferred* given over (as a punishment)

138

1 When my love swears that she is made of truth
2 I do believe her, though I know she lies,
3 That she might think me some untutored youth,
4 Unlearnèd in the world's false subtilties.
5 Thus vainly thinking that she thinks me young,
  Although she knows my days are past the best,
7 Simply I credit her false-speaking tongue;
  On both sides thus is simple truth suppressed.
9 But wherefore says she not she is unjust?
10 And wherefore say not I that I am old?
11 O, love's best habit is in seeming trust,
12 And age in love loves not to have years told.
13   Therefore I lie with her and she with me,
14   And in our faults by lies we flattered be.

See also the alternate version in 138a.
1 *made of truth* (1) totally honest, (2) utterly faithful **2** *lies* (playing on the physical sense invoked in l. 13) **3** *That* so that **4** *subtilties* guile, craftiness **5** *vainly* (1) pointlessly, (2) self-indulgently **7** *Simply* (1) naively, (2) unhesitatingly **9** *unjust* (1) untruthful, (2) unfaithful **11** *love's . . . is* love looks best when dressed **12** *told* (1) counted, (2) revealed **13** *lie . . . her* (1) sleep with her, (2) tell her lies **14** *flattered be* are comfortably deceived

138a

When my love swears that she is made of truth,
I do believe her, though I know she lies,
That she might think me some untutored youth,
Unskillful in the world's false forgeries.
Thus vainly thinking that she thinks me young,
Although I know my years be past the best,
I smiling credit her false-speaking tongue,
Outfacing faults in love with love's ill rest.   8
But wherefore says my love that she is young?   9
And wherefore say not I that I am old?   10
O, love's best habit is a soothing tongue,
And age in love loves not to have years told.
   Therefore I'll lie with love, and love with me,
   Since that our faults in love thus smothered be.

This version of Sonnet 138 was published in *The Passionate Pilgrim*, 1599, a collection of twenty poems all credited to Shakespeare, though only this, a version of Sonnet 144, and versions of three poems from *Love's Labor's Lost* are indisputably his. Of these five, only this includes variants revealing that the poem underwent significant revision.
8 *ill rest* (1) restlessness, (2) sleeplessness **9–10** *wherefore . . . old* i.e., why can she say she is young, and I can't admit that I am old

139

1 O, call not me to justify the wrong
That thy unkindness lays upon my heart;
3 Wound me not with thine eye but with thy tongue;
4 Use power with power, and slay me not by art.
5 Tell me thou lov'st elsewhere; but in my sight,
6 Dear heart, forbear to glance thine eye aside;
7 What need'st thou wound with cunning when thy might
8 Is more than my o'erpressed defense can bide?
9 Let me excuse thee: ah, my love well knows
10 Her pretty looks have been mine enemies;
And therefore from my face she turns my foes,
That they elsewhere might dart their injuries –
13   Yet do not so; but since I am near slain,
   Kill me outright with looks and rid my pain.

---

1 *call not me* don't ask me 3 *with . . . eye* i.e., by letting me see you looking at other men; *with . . . tongue* i.e., only tell me about it 4 *Use . . . with power* use your power as strongly as you can; *art* artfulness, *cunning* (see l. 7) 5 *elsewhere* somebody else 6 *glance . . . aside* look sidelong (at someone else) 7 *What* why 8 *o'erpressed* overwhelmed; *bide* endure 9 *excuse thee* i.e., *justify the wrong* after all (see l. 1) 13 *near* nearly

140

Be wise as thou art cruel: do not press   1
My tongue-tied patience with too much disdain,
Lest sorrow lend me words, and words express
The manner of my pity-wanting pain.   4
If I might teach thee wit, better it were,   5
Though not to love, yet, love, to tell me so;   6
As testy sick men, when their deaths be near,   7
No news but health from their physicians know.
For if I should despair, I should grow mad,
And in my madness might speak ill of thee: 10
Now this ill-wresting world is grown so bad   11
Mad slanderers by mad ears believèd be.   12
   That I may not be so, nor thou belied,   13
   Bear thine eyes straight, though thy proud heart go wide.   14

---

1 *Be . . . cruel* (1) be just as wise as you are cruel, (2) be wise, since you are cruel; *press* (1) oppress, (2) pressure   4 *manner* nature; *pity-wanting* (1) without your pity, (2) eager for pity   5 *wit* wisdom, good sense   6 *so* i.e., that you do   7 *testy* peevish   11 *ill-wresting* twisting everything to its worst sense   12 *mad ears* i.e., the witless hearers of this *ill-wresting world*   13 *so* i.e., both a *Mad slanderer* and *believèd*   14 *proud heart* (1) arrogant spirit, (2) lecherous desire (compare "lust" as "proud," Sonnet 129, l. 11); *wide* astray

141

In faith, I do not love thee with mine eyes,
2 For they in thee a thousand errors note;
But 'tis my heart that loves what they despise,
4 Who in despite of view is pleased to dote.
Nor are mine ears with thy tongue's tune delighted,
6 Nor tender feeling to base touches prone,
Nor taste, nor smell, desire to be invited
8 To any sensual feast with thee alone;
9 But my five wits nor my five senses can
10 Dissuade one foolish heart from serving thee,
11 Who leaves unswayed the likeness of a man,
Thy proud heart's slave and vassal wretch to be:
13   Only my plague thus far I count my gain,
14   That she that makes me sin awards me pain.

---

2 *errors* faults 4 *Who . . . view* which despite what is seen 6 *tender feeling*
my refined sense of touch; *base touches* (1) coarse caresses, (2) unworthy as-
pects 8 *sensual feast* feast of the senses 9 *But* but neither; *five wits* (the in-
tellectual powers, as opposed to the senses, usually enumerated as common
sense, imagination, fantasy, judgment, memory) 11 *leaves . . . man* i.e.,
ceases to govern the body, leaving it the mere semblance of a man 13
Only . . . plague nevertheless, my suffering 14 *That . . . pain* i.e., that the
pain is inflicted by her

142

Love is my sin, and thy dear virtue hate,
Hate of my sin, grounded on sinful loving.   2
O, but with mine compare thou thine own state,   3
And thou shalt find it merits not reproving;
Or if it do, not from those lips of thine,
That have profaned their scarlet ornaments   6
And sealed false bonds of love as oft as mine,   7
Robbed others' beds' revenues of their rents.   8
Be it lawful I love thee as thou lov'st those
Whom thine eyes woo as mine importune thee: 10
Root pity in thy heart, that, when it grows,   11
Thy pity may deserve to pitied be.   12
   If thou dost seek to have what thou dost hide,   13
   By self-example mayst thou be denied.   14

---

2 *grounded . . . loving* i.e., (1) my sin involves a love that is unsanctioned, lustful, adulterous, (2) your hatred derives from your own sinful love, lustful, promiscuous, and adulterous 3 *mine* my state 6 *scarlet ornaments* (the *lips*, compared to seals on a document) 7 *as mine* as mine have done 8 *Robbed . . . rents* i.e., stolen away other women's husbands (the *rents* are what is owed to the *revenue*, or wealth, of the marriage bed – both fidelity and offspring) 11 *pity* (1) sympathy, (2) sexual compliance 12 *Thy . . . be* your pity will then deserve my pity 13 *what . . . hide* what you withhold, *pity* 14 *denied* refused

143

1 Lo, as a careful housewife runs to catch
2 One of her feathered creatures broke away,
3 Sets down her babe, and makes all swift dispatch
  In pursuit of the thing she would have stay;
5 Whilst her neglected child holds her in chase,
6 Cries to catch her whose busy care is bent
  To follow that which flies before her face,
8 Not prizing her poor infant's discontent:
  So runn'st thou after that which flies from thee,
10 Whilst I, thy babe, chase thee afar behind;
11 But if thou catch thy hope, turn back to me
  And play the mother's part, kiss me, be kind.
13   So will I pray that thou mayst have thy Will,
     If thou turn back and my loud crying still.

---

1 *careful* (1) provident, (2) prudent, (3) anxious; *housewife* (spelled "huswife" in Q and pronounced "hussif") 2 *feathered creatures* barnyard fowls (perhaps also implying that the rival lover is a dandy – feathers were a notorious feature of male fancy dress in the period); *broke* which has broken (out of its pen) 3 *dispatch* haste 5 *holds . . . chase* chases her 6 *bent* (1) determined, (2) turned aside (from the *child*) 8 *prizing* concerned about 11 *thy hope* what you pursue (the *Will* in l. 13) 13 *thy Will* (1) the rival lover named Will (italicized and capitalized in Q; see Sonnets 135 and 136), (2) your desire, (3) me (also named Will, with all the overtones implied in Sonnet 136, l. 14)

144

Two loves I have, of comfort and despair,   1
Which like two spirits do suggest me still: 2
The better angel is a man right fair,   3
The worser spirit a woman colored ill.   4
To win me soon to hell, my female evil   5
Tempteth my better angel from my side,
And would corrupt my saint to be a devil,
Wooing his purity with her foul pride.   8
And whether that my angel be turned fiend
Suspect I may, yet not directly tell;   10
But being both from me, both to each friend,   11
I guess one angel in another's hell.   12
    Yet this shall I ne'er know, but live in doubt,
    Till my bad angel fire my good one out.   14

Another version of this sonnet, with minor variants, appears in *The Passionate Pilgrim,* 1599. See the headnote to Sonnet 138a.
1 *loves* lovers (see Sonnets 40–42) **2** *suggest* (1) prompt, (2) tempt; *still* always **3** *right fair* (1) very beautiful, (2) entirely fair in complexion, (3) completely honorable **4** *colored ill* of a bad – i.e., dark – complexion **5–6** *my . . . angel* i.e., the good and bad angels, instead of prompting the poet, tempt each other and abandon him **8** *pride* (1) display, stylish appearance, (2) lust **10** *directly* (1) immediately, (2) entirely **11** *from me* gone from me; *to each friend* friend to each other **12** *hell* (slang for the vagina) **14** *fire . . . out* (1) expel my good angel, (2) infect my good angel with venereal disease

145

Those lips that Love's own hand did make
Breathed forth the sound that said "I hate"
To me that languished for her sake;
But when she saw my woeful state,
5 Straight in her heart did mercy come,
6 Chiding that tongue that ever sweet
7 Was used in giving gentle doom,
8 And taught it thus anew to greet:
"I hate" she altered with an end
10 That followed it as gentle day
Doth follow night, who, like a fiend,
From heaven to hell is flown away.
13   "I hate" from hate away she threw,
   And saved my life, saying "not you."

Like Sonnets 99 and 126, an anomaly, both in form and tone. Its authenticity has been questioned, but the apparent pun on the name of Shakespeare's wife, Anne Hathaway, in the final couplet suggests that it is in fact an early poem of Shakespeare's. Its inclusion in the collection is puzzling, but its placement in the sequence, whether by Shakespeare or by an editor who had read the poems with great care, is surely intentional: it mediates in a light-hearted way between two very serious sonnets concerned with good and evil, heaven and hell.

5 *Straight* immediately   6–7 *ever . . . used* (1) always used to be sweet, (2) was always sweetly employed   7 *gentle doom* (1) kind judgment, (2) a light sentence   8 *greet* say to me   13 *hate away* (apparently punning on "Hathaway," Shakespeare's wife's maiden name)

146

Poor soul, the center of my sinful earth,   1
[Pressed by] these rebel powers that thee array,   2
Why dost thou pine within and suffer dearth,   3
Painting thy outward walls so costly gay?   4
Why so large cost, having so short a lease,   5
Dost thou upon thy fading mansion spend?
Shall worms, inheritors of this excess,
Eat up thy charge? Is this thy body's end?   8
Then, soul, live thou upon thy servant's loss,
And let that pine to aggravate thy store;   10
Buy terms divine in selling hours of dross;   11
Within be fed, without be rich no more: 12
    So shalt thou feed on Death, that feeds on men,
    And Death once dead, there's no more dying then.

---

1 *earth* i.e., body   2 *Pressed by* oppressed by, hard pressed by (Q repeats *My sinful earth*, which cannot be correct. *Pressed by* is arbitrarily chosen from among several hundred plausible readings proposed since the eighteenth century.); *rebel powers* i.e., the flesh, the passions; *array* (1) order, (2) clothe, (3) afflict   3 *pine* (1) starve, (2) sorrow   4 *Painting . . . gay* i.e., dressing your body so expensively and fashionably   5 *cost* expense   8 *thy charge* (1) the body you are in charge of, (2) what has cost you so much   10 *that* the *servant*, the *body*; *aggravate* increase, improve; *store* supplies   11 *terms divine* (1) heavenly periods of time, (2) a new lease on God's terms; *dross* waste   12 *without* externally

147

1 My love is as a fever, longing still
2 For that which longer nurseth the disease,
3 Feeding on that which doth preserve the ill,
4 Th' uncertain sickly appetite to please.
  My reason, the physician to my love,
6 Angry that his prescriptions are not kept,
7 Hath left me, and I desperate now approve
8 Desire is death, which physic did except.
9 Past cure I am, now reason is past care,
10 And frantic-mad with evermore unrest;
  My thoughts and my discourse as madmen's are,
12 At random from the truth vainly expressed:
13   For I have sworn thee fair, and thought thee bright,
    Who art as black as hell, as dark as night.

---

1 *still* incessantly 2 *nurseth* nourishes, prolongs 3 *ill* (1) illness, (2) evil
4 *uncertain* indecisive, inconstant 6 *kept* followed 7 *approve* (1) prove
through my example, (2) learn from experience 8 *Desire . . . except* that sex-
ual desire, which the physician *reason* forbade me, is tantamount to death
9 *is . . . care* no longer cares about me 10 *evermore* (1) constant, (2) increas-
ing 12 *At random* totally missing; *vainly* pointlessly, senselessly 13 *fair* (1)
beautiful, (2) just, (3) honest (as with *black* and *dark* in l. 14, the primary
senses are moral, not visual)

148

O me, what eyes hath love put in my head,
Which have no correspondence with true sight;   2
Or, if they have, where is my judgment fled,
That censures falsely what they see aright?   4
If that be fair whereon my false eyes dote,   5
What means the world to say it is not so?
If it be not, then love doth well denote   7
Love's eye is not so true as all men's no.   8
How can it? O, how can love's eye be true,
That is so vexed with watching and with tears?   10
No marvel then though I mistake my view: 11
The sun itself sees not till heaven clears.
    O cunning love, with tears thou keep'st me blind,
    Lest eyes well-seeing thy foul faults should find.

---

2 *have . . . sight* (1) do not see what corresponds to reality, (2) are not like eyes that see truly   4 *censures* judges (not derogatory); *falsely* (1) incorrectly, (2) dishonestly   5 *fair* (1) beautiful, (2) honorable   7 *love . . . denote* the fact that I love clearly indicates   8 *eye* (punning on "ay")   10 *vexed* afflicted; *watching* sleeplessness   11 *marvel* wonder; *my view* what I see

149

Canst thou, O cruel, say I love thee not
2 When I against myself with thee partake?
3 Do I not think on thee when I forgot
4 Am of myself, all tyrant for thy sake?
Who hateth thee that I do call my friend?
On whom frown'st thou that I do fawn upon?
7 Nay, if thou lour'st on me, do I not spend
8 Revenge upon myself with present moan?
What merit do I in myself respect
10 That is so proud thy service to despise,
11 When all my best doth worship thy defect,
Commanded by the motion of thine eyes?
　　But, love, hate on, for now I know thy mind;
14 　　Those that can see thou lov'st, and I am blind.

---

2 *partake* join forces　**3–4** *forgot . . . myself* forget myself completely, am totally oblivious of myself　**4** *all tyrant* (1) I become a tyrant to myself, (2) you who are utterly tyrannous　**7** *thou lour'st* you frown　**8** *present moan* immediate grief　**10** *so . . . despise* so proud as to despise serving you　**11** *all . . . defect* everything that is best in me worships your imperfections　**14** *Those . . . lov'st* i.e., you love those who see only the external you

150

O, from what power hast thou this powerful might
With insufficiency my heart to sway? 2
To make me give the lie to my true sight 3
And swear that brightness doth not grace the day? 4
Whence hast thou this becoming of things ill, 5
That in the very refuse of thy deeds 6
There is such strength and warrantise of skill 7
That in my mind thy worst all best exceeds?
Who taught thee how to make me love thee more,
The more I hear and see just cause of hate? 10
O, though I love what others do abhor, 11
With others thou shouldst not abhor my state: 12
   If thy unworthiness raised love in me,
    More worthy I to be beloved of thee.

---

2 *insufficiency* your defects 3 *give . . . to* call a liar 4 *brightness . . . day* i.e., but (the lady's) darkness does 5 *becoming . . . ill* power to make bad things seem attractive 6 *the . . . deeds* (1) the least of your actions, (2) the vilest of your deeds 7 *warrantise of skill* assurance of ability 11, 12 *abhor* (punning on "whore") 12 *With others* (1) by sleeping with others, (2) as others do

151

Love is too young to know what conscience is;
2 Yet who knows not conscience is born of love?
3 Then, gentle cheater, urge not my amiss,
4 Lest guilty of my faults thy sweet self prove.
For, thou betraying me, I do betray
6 My nobler part to my gross body's treason;
My soul doth tell my body that he may
8 Triumph in love; flesh stays no farther reason,
9 But, rising at thy name, doth point out thee
10 As his triumphant prize. Proud of this pride,
11 He is contented thy poor drudge to be,
To stand in thy affairs, fall by thy side.
13   No want of conscience hold it that I call
     Her "love" for whose dear love I rise and fall.

---

2 *conscience* sexual awareness, guilty knowledge (as opposed to the sense of moral scruples in l. 1)   3 *cheater* deceiver; *urge . . . amiss* don't charge me with misbehavior   4 *Lest . . . prove* (1) lest you turn out to be guilty of the same faults I am, (2) lest you turn out to be responsible for my faults   6 *nobler part* reason, soul   8 *stays* waits for   9 *rising* (1) growing erect, (2) rebelling, (3) conjured up   10 *Proud . . . pride* (1) aroused by this sexual excitement, (2) glorying in this erection   11 *poor drudge* i.e., sexual servant   13 *want* lack; *conscience* (in the senses of both ll. 1 and 2)

152

In loving thee thou know'st I am forsworn,   1
But thou art twice forsworn, to me love swearing;   2
In act thy bed vow broke, and new faith torn   3
In vowing new hate after new love bearing.   4
But why of two oaths' breach do I accuse thee
When I break twenty? I am perjured most,
For all my vows are oaths but to misuse thee,   7
And all my honest faith in thee is lost;   8
For I have sworn deep oaths of thy deep kindness,
Oaths of thy love, thy truth, thy constancy;   10
And, to enlighten thee, gave eyes to blindness,   11
Or made them swear against the thing they see;   12
   For I have sworn thee fair: more perjured eye,   13
   To swear against the truth so foul a lie.

---

1 *forsworn* untrue to someone else (another lover, or if we take the sonnet to be autobiographical, to Anne Hathaway)   2 *twice forsworn* (either untrue to both her husband and the friend, if the poem is one of the group referring to the love triangle, or untrue to the husband and to the poet himself)   3 *act* sexual activity; *bed vow* marriage vow; *torn* (the image is of a contract torn up)   4 *bearing* (1) professing, (2) supporting (in bed)   7 *misuse* (1) abuse, (2) deceive, (3) misrepresent   8 *honest ... in* integrity through   11 *enlighten thee* make you bright or fair; *gave ... blindness* (1) gave up my eyes in favor of blindness, (2) made my blindness the source of my vision of you   12 *swear against* falsely deny   13 *eye* (punning on "I")

final couplet
for sequence ⟵ ⟵

153

1 Cupid laid by his brand and fell asleep:
2 A maid of Dian's this advantage found
  And his love-kindling fire did quickly steep
4 In a cold valley-fountain of that ground;
  Which borrowed from this holy fire of Love
6 A dateless lively heat, still to endure,
7 And grew a seething bath, which yet men prove
8 Against strange maladies a sovereign cure.
  But at my mistress' eye Love's brand new fired,
10 The boy for trial needs would touch my breast;
11 I, sick withal, the help of bath desired
12 And thither hied, a sad distempered guest,
      But found no cure: the bath for my help lies
      Where Cupid got new fire, my mistress' eyes.

The final two poems, modeled on epigrams from the classic collection now referred to as the Greek Anthology, bring the sequence to a conclusion by invoking familiar classic literary tropes. Though they are not part of the narrative, they deal lightly and playfully with themes and images that fill the previous sonnets, and contextualize the sequence within a long poetic heritage.

1 *brand* torch   2 *A . . . Dian's* one of Diana's virgin nymphs; *advantage* opportunity   4 *of . . . ground* nearby   6 *A dateless* an eternal; *still* always   7 *grew* became; *seething bath* (perhaps alluding to the "sweating tubs" used in the treatment of syphilis, the disease of love); *yet . . . prove* people still find to be   8 *strange* (1) extreme, (2) unusual; *sovereign* powerful   10 *for . . . touch* had to test it upon   11 *withal* from that; *bath* (the curative *bath* of l. 7)   12 *hied* hurried; *a sad distempered* (1) a sadly diseased, (2) an unhappy, ill

154

The little Love god, lying once asleep,
Laid by his side his heart-inflaming brand,   2
Whilst many nymphs that vowed chaste life to keep
Came tripping by; but in her maiden hand
The fairest votary took up that fire   5
Which many legions of true hearts had warmed;
And so the general of hot desire   7
Was, sleeping, by a virgin hand disarmed.
This brand she quenchèd in a cool well by,   9
Which from Love's fire took heat perpetual,   10
Growing a bath and healthful remedy   11
For men diseased; but I, my mistress' thrall,   12
    Came there for cure, and this by that I prove:
    Love's fire heats water, water cools not love.

---

2 *brand* torch 5 *votary* nymph of Diana, vowed to chastity 7 *general* commander 9 *by* nearby 11 *Growing* becoming 12 *thrall* slave

Index of First Lines

The figures in parentheses refer to the number of the sonnet.